M000208572

Step On It

One Woman's Adventure in the Race Across America

Amy Shonstrom

as told to Michael Shonstrom

Copyright © 2013 Shonstrom Research Associates, LLC
Publisher

All rights Reserved

ISBN – 13: 978-0615927947

ISBN – 10: 0615927947

DEDICATION

This book is dedicated to my late Mother, Adelaine, and to my wife, Amy. The two are birds of a feather. They never met, but would have made a great pair.

CONTENTS

Acknowledgements

I have always loved citizen racing. To me, any event that gets broad participation by the average Joe, the next door neighbor or your Mom, creates a community of shared experience that's rewarding and fun. Increasingly, the endurance end of the event spectrum has become a big draw. From marathons to iron man triathlons, and cross country ski loppets to hundred mile runs and endurance bike races, the number of athletes attempting these races has been increasing, especially women. It seems the more suffering and misery one endures, the more satisfying the accomplishment of finishing becomes.

So to begin this book, I would like to acknowledge all those weekend athletes, who took themselves out of their comfort zones and pulled on running shoes or cleats or ski boots and took on the challenge. Among them is Amy, and without her, this book would not have been written. She not only provided me the narrative, but was my inspiration in so many ways. She accepted the challenge of the race, trained for it, raised money for it and rode it. And while doing all that, even though I did my best to look after her, she also looked after me. Measured by her tenacity, her toughness and her heart, she ranks as one of my all-time heroes, which, because I'm married to her is a very good thing.

Along with Amy, I would also like to recognize all the family members and friends who contributed to Love Sweat & Gears through the team's charity, LiveWell Colorado.

I also would like to thank my son Erik for his encouragement and suggestions in the writing of this book and to thank Jerry Miller for his editing. Jerry didn't get to the last third of the book, so any mistakes there are on me.

"We tend to have very self-limiting beliefs about what's possible. I used to think I couldn't go on a big adventure because I wasn't 6'3" and bearded. But I think we could actually take much bolder steps than we tend to believe we can." *Roz Savage, multiple world record holder, solo ocean rowing.*

"Julie and I plan to be creative to help her make it." *Ann Lantz said in speaking to Dina Hannah regarding Amy at the start of the 2012 Race Across America.*

"There was an opinion on the team that you were in over your head", *Jim Harper said in a conversation with Amy after the race.*

Chapter 1

The Death Zone

The RV had reached Prescott, Arizona around noon on Sunday, June 17th. We were now 24 hours into the Race Across America and most of our mileage had been through portions of the predictably hot and dry northern Sonoran Desert, which stretched 360 miles from Borrego Springs to our present location - about 18 hours on the bike. Racers have named this area the "death zone" because of the toll it takes on competitors. This year has been no different as it had already claimed all the 2 person relay teams that had started three days earlier along with a half dozen solo riders.

Our team and crew had professed the belief that we had the ability to set a new women's 4 person relay record and at the outset that was our objective. But we had not picked up the crucial tailwinds through the California desert that had propelled the record setters; a team from California named the Raw Milk Cats, which left us 3 hours behind the pace they set in 2011.

Dina Hannah, my riding partner and I had taken over from our two Love Sweat & Gears cohorts, Ann Lantz and Julie Lyons, and would be riding the next 95 mile segment up the Mogollon Rim, which marks the southern edge of the Colorado Plateau ending in Flagstaff at 7,005 feet in elevation. We were still feeling the effects of racing for 5 hours earlier in the day in heat that exceeded

100° and climbing 2,200 feet. We had finished that ride in Congress, AZ, at 10:28 am. But what we would be facing over the next 6 hours would be intensified by the asphalt radiating heat back at us and a route that included 5,000 feet of serious climbing over 2 mountain passes. In Prescott, temperatures had pushed up to 107°.

Dina had been first up on the bike on the way out of town on, Highway 89 toward Jerome, and I was being shuttled in the Audi Q5, my support vehicle. When we turned on the Pioneer Parkway, we hit a construction zone where the pavement was torn up. Dina stopped there, her crew picked her up and they went on ahead. Our RAAM race instructions required riders to be shuttled by vehicle for 3 miles until we cleared the construction area. It was my turn to ride and in a decision now lost to time, the Audi stopped to put me out on the road with about a mile of torn up pavement still to go.

Paul, one of my support crew, jumped out of the car and went to the rack in the rear to grab my bike. When he opened the door, the outside heat immediately challenged the air conditioned interior. He wheeled the bike in front of the car and I got out following. It was like stepping into a furnace room. I took the bike from him, threw my leg over, secured my cleat in the pedal, pushed off and began to pedal cautiously as I made my way along a roadway surface featuring sharp furrows from an asphalt milling machine that had removed the top layer. I concentrated on avoiding cracks, loose chunks or sharp edges so as not to risk a puncture and after several minutes of riding, I hit smooth pavement.

The glare of the sun overhead radiated heat on my back and the pavement reflected it from below. But, I pushed thoughts of heat, construction zones and the climbing ahead as far out of my head as I could, settled into my aero bars and tried to pick up a 90 rpm tempo as I took on my pull.

The countryside was a flat high chaparral with a few commercial areas and moderate traffic. I could see the Black Hills mountain range in the distance as Dina and I started out trading 3 mile pulls, but after an hour, the road tilted up and we began a more serious climb up Hayman Canyon to the pass between Hickey and Mingus Mountains. Heat waves shimmered off the road.

By my third pull, my crew and I decided to cut my efforts to 2 miles at a time. This still meant about 15 minutes of riding each time as the increased grade reduced our speed. This was the distance that our other team members, Ann and Julie, had ridden when they did this section in the 870 mile, Race Across the West (RAW), two years before.

Using their experience as a guide, it seemed to be a good choice. Dina, who was 14 years younger and was not as affected by the heat, chose 3 mile pulls. Even with the shorter distance, I found myself beginning to feel the effects of the heat by the end of each turn and at some point, a dull headache developed. I had never been a great hot weather competitor and it was proving to be the case again. A niggling fear of failure emerged. I was beginning to suffer too soon.

As I climbed up Hayman Canyon, I battled with trying to shut out the messages my body was sending by concentrating on a steady tempo and thinking about something cool. Earlier in the day, an ice cold fudgesicle had captured my imagination, but it now seemed a paltry palliative and failed to measure up to the heat index. A new mental "mirage" was needed.

 It finally came to me as I stood on the side of the road waiting to take over from Dina next to a highway mileage marker that stated, "Jerome 10", and underneath, "Flagstaff 69". The Pioneer Highway was also named The Prescott Jerome Waterway. Why that was eluded me. There was a dry wash by the road that could hardly be called a waterway.

However, the idea of water and of being on a large body of water was enticing. I began to fixate on paddling along on a stand up paddleboard surrounded by water in a blue lagoon wafted by cool breezes. I had never done it before, but had seen the sport featured in some of the women's sport apparel catalogs that come in the mail. Now it became my new fantasy; an image to try and trick my brain into ignoring the heat.

The Toyota came around a bend in the road with Dina in front. It took effort to throw my leg over the seat and click in. As she drew near, I started out and as she came by me I heard her say something derogatory about the heat. I zoned it out and concentrated on getting the energy to move. We rode together for four or five pedal strokes and then I was alone. I dropped into my aero bars, picked up a rhythm and tried to think of paddling my board on a large expanse of cool water. I had a small laugh as I wondered whether my mirage fantasy would be fodder for a "New Yorker" cartoon of someone crawling across the desert who looks up to see a paddleboard rental booth blocking his way.

The road up the Hayman was going almost due east and the sun came down directly on my back. I was perspiring freely, but it evaporated so quickly my exposed skin seemed dry. As my heart rate increased, each pulse created a corresponding beat of dull pain in my head.

We slugged our way up the 4% grade trading pulls out in the heat with respites back in the car. During those moments, I did what I could to cool myself down with ice water and a cool wash cloth over my flushed face. I was on the bike when we reached the first summit at a place called the Potato Patch.

Dina took over there and proceeded to do the entire 3,200 foot descent over the next 15 miles through the old mining town of Jerome, which hangs on the side of the mountain, toward the outskirts of Cottonwood. It was all downhill with lots of switchbacks requiring minimal pedaling effort and a lengthy section that went through traffic in the town which is a draw for tourists. This gave me extra minutes of recovery time.

Several miles below Jerome, the road flattened out near Clarkdale. I took over from Dina there and rode into the town of Cottonwood.

Over the 15 months of preparation since I agreed to join the team, the confidence I had built in my ability to finish the race had been high, but there was always a scintilla of fear lurking in the back of my mind that I wouldn't be able to make it. And as we rode toward Flagstaff and into a cauldron of heat that afternoon, it would come back to visit me.

My confidence was as high as ever, but my husband, Mike, had pointed out to me that in staying with the vehicle meeting points that had been planned, Dina and I would be riding nearly 12 hours in the daytime heat with only 3 hours of recovery time. This would include the Hayman climb we had just done followed by Oak Creek Canyon that we now faced.

Months ago at the beginning of the year, Mike had attended a Crew Seminar offered by the race organizers along with the two crew leaders. It was there that four hour ride segments were suggested as optimal for 4 person relay teams. It was believed that a schedule of 4 hours on, 4 hours off, was the best equation to provide adequate recovery time and at the same time maximize speed on the road.

The 4 hour mantra had been corroborated by conversations that I had held with members of the Raw Milk Cats team, whose record we were trying to beat, and several riders from the 4 man Mucho Gusto team from Denver who rode in 2005. I spoke with the legendary Fuzzy Mitchell, namesake of an award given out each year by RAAM organizers to the best crew. Fuzzy, who had ridden the race himself on three 4-man teams and had been a Crew Chief numerous times, most recently for the Raw Milk Cat's effort, believed that stopping for exchanges at the 4 hour mark was a gospel not to be broken.

For this day, such was not to be the case. When we hit Cottonwood, we had been on the bike 2 hours 20 minutes since

Prescott. From Cottonwood to Flagstaff, it would be another 53 miles of steady climbing before the route flattened out for the last 10 miles, and would require another 3 ½ hours more of cycling. The uphill grade of the road coming out of Cottonwood was initially moderate, but we stayed with shorter pulls. When we reached Oak Creek Canyon, starting in Sedona, we would be on a 5% grade for the first 13 miles, and then would hit the 8% Sterling Switchbacks for another 3 miles before the run into Flagstaff. To put this into perspective, the maximum desirable grade for US Highways is 6%. When the pitch gets to that level and above, it gets your attention.

I thought about yesterday back in California, when I began my very first ride. I had this image of being a small speck on this immensely long road a huge distance away from my final destination. It seemed so far away, an unimaginably daunting journey. I now looked at the remaining miles to Flagstaff that way. It almost seemed beyond my grasp given the heat, yet we'd only been racing for one day. The demands of the race were hard enough physically, but with the heat it was becoming a mental challenge as well.

One of the Mucho Gusto riders that I had talked to, Shannon Gillespie, had run into difficulties of his own during this part of the race. He was about 20 years younger than I, an experienced cyclist who had been trained for the race by Chris Carmichael. He had chosen to fuel with a liquid food for endurance athletes. But despite the liquid diet, he apparently didn't hydrate enough and succumbed to the heat. He began to cramp and then went down with heat stroke. He had to be pulled off the road, after he began vomiting, and momentarily blacked out. The team's RV then took him to the hospital in Flagstaff for an IV infusion. He ended up missing two of his 4 hour legs, leaving the team with 3 riders during the better part of a similarly hot day.

This is not an experience I wanted to share. I didn't want to leave the road on a gurney. I didn't want to burn myself up so that I would be unable to recover. I wanted to be a trusted part of the team.

But the sun's rays were unrelenting. At one point, Jim Harper, a photographer that had supported us with pictures and videos for our website and Facebook page, caught me with his video camera and asked how I was doing.

In the footage, I looked stressed, my face was flushed and I had an unattractive smear of zinc oxide on my nose.

"It's hard," I replied, "but I'm doing it. Quitting is not an option".

And it wasn't.

But it was damn hard. As I rode, I repeatedly pushed myself to the edge of my endurance. Was I at risk of reaching the point that Shannon had during his race? As negative thoughts entered my head, I would try to push them away and focus on the paddleboard in the cool lagoon.

Beyond Cottonwood, Highway 89 became a divided road. We were in the same rolling terrain we saw starting out in Prescott. There was no vegetation over three feet high. No shade. It was windless. Even our forward progress didn't offer much of a cooling effect. Sedona was still 15 miles away. It marked the start of the Oak Creek Canyon. All told, we would gain 3,744 feet from Cottonwood. By now my face was flushed bright red. My body was now coping with two demands, supplying energy to my muscles and trying to keep my inner body temperature normal. If my core temperature rose too high, there wouldn't be enough blood supply for the muscles and I would start to cramp and go in the same downward spiral Shannon experienced.

After the race he admitted, "My body just shut down. I couldn't keep anything in my stomach and was nauseous for 12 hours. I thought I was going to have to quit. I broke down and cried."

Between each ride, I thought of Shannon's demise while I worked on getting my body temperature down. My crew, Paul and Richie looked around to make sure I was taking care of myself and offered whatever support they thought I might need. Support crews were expected to make sure their riders hydrated, ate something and make sure they cooled off between rides. This responsibility fell primarily on whoever was navigating. But the race was on secondary roads, so navigators spent most of each ride looking down the road, checking the route book and GPS to make sure we made all the right turns. The follow vehicles also were equipped with radios, so communicating with the crew in Dina's follow vehicle as to the distance to the next the next relay exchange point; and once established, the description of it occupied them as well.

As a result, I was in charge and I milked each moment off the bike for as much unbothered rest and recovery as I could. Drinking was easy, eating was harder. A good friend, Dean Smith, an 85 year old world record holding runner and rower that my husband, Mike, competes with, had supplied me with a Shaklee Performance electrolyte replacement drink product that I liked. For food, I nibbled at peanut butter and jelly sandwiches on white bread, which were becoming my go-to food, Niki Parkhill's famous trail mix, Honey Stinger waffles, pieces of Payday bars and my other favorite - handfuls of salty potato chips. It was probably not the menu that the performance food companies had in mind, but it worked for me.

Also out of concern for the hot weather, I had swallowed a bunch of salt tablets. What with the need to constantly drink water to keep my body fluids and blood pressure up, it resulted in a need to pee frequently, a seemingly unimportant issue except under these temperature conditions, it was an added annoyance. The experience was draining (yes, I said that). RAAM is not an environment where the racer gestures a timeout signal and everything stops for a socially acceptable potty break. One goes where the vehicle stops for a rider exchange. There are few civilities.

The fact that my neighbor's young son was my on my crew gave me a momentary sense of shyness, but that passed quickly. The idea of privacy in an unexposed spot proved to be a luxury. There was also the worry that I might be peeing too much, that my body wasn't retaining enough liquids.   Endurance racing was virgin territory for me and each new sensation raised a new question.

The heat remained oppressive even though it was afternoon now. Each time back in the Audi, I would repeat the routine – drink, use a wet towel to cool down, nibble on some food and then get ready to get out on the bike again, sometimes preceded by a preliminary excursion in the sage brush for a pee. Each time back on the bike, there was a moment of trepidation as I waited for Dina to reach me. Will I be able to do this? And each time out my legs responded. They felt heavy, I never felt I could settle into a comfortable tempo that cyclists like to find, but the legs still worked. The sun was relentless, the traffic on the highway was an irritant, my headache was a distraction, but my legs continued to respond. It's a seeming paradox, but despite what my body was enduring, and what my mind was telling me, I kept turning the pedals over.

There is an inspiration for perseverance. Not far to the northwest, in 1849, a wagon train of pioneers passed through southern Nevada on what they thought was a short cut from Provo to California gold fields that avoided the notorious Donner Pass. In that train was a wispy, 80 lb. woman named Juliet Brier. She had three children and would sometimes carry the youngest one on her back or in her arms while holding another child's hand. The route her company took led them straight into the middle of Death Valley. Four men died on that trip.

Juliet, the only woman in the group, ended up nursing her husband, cooking, harnessing, packing up and driving the oxen after abandoning the wagons. In his book, <u>Men to Match My Mountains</u>, Irving Stone relates that on reaching a source of water at Furnace Creek, she was asked if she wanted to stay there and wait for a rescue party. She replied emphatically, no! And stated in no uncertain terms that each step she took would be towards California. I was going in the other direction, towards Annapolis, but my resolve was just as strong.

Before we reached Sedona, when Dina came up alongside at an exchange, she said, "I don't think I can do this much longer".

That was hard to imagine. Dina, who I considered the war horse of our team given her endurance racing credentials, is struggling? She had the added burden of a faulty air conditioner in the Toyota. It wasn't working in the rear and she had to compensate with ice bags while her crew spritzed her from water filled spray bottles. But if anyone should be considered the weak link in the chain, it was me. Yet here was proof that I was no more vulnerable than anyone else. And while it didn't make me feel any better physically, at least I knew my suffering wasn't exclusive.

"The heat was debilitating" I later told a crew from The NBC Nightly News. We were to be the subject of a public interest story that they would broadcast on their program later that summer. Michelle Franzen and a film crew had been following us from the start and recording our experience.

"At one point I said to myself, 'I'm cooked'", I added, "' am I going to have to get off my bike and sit on the side of the road until the sun goes down?'".

In that video piece, Dina and I stood arm in arm. She was shaking her head in agreement as I talked about the heat.

"The heat was overwhelming", Dina said in another part of the segment. "At one point, the car's thermometer only said 102°", she continued, "and I ride in hot weather, but this is the only time I have ever burned my fingers on my gear shifters!"

At 4:45 pm, 58 miles out of Prescott, we passed through Sedona and I remember thinking, this is a great vacation destination, I should be looking around to take in the ambiance and the views, but all I could think about was the hurt locker I was in. All my senses were tuned to my body's reaction to the heat and the physical demands of pedaling the bike up the road. The scenic landscape, as dramatic as it was, the town, as picturesque as it is, escaped me.

Past Sedona, the road tipped up again and we began to pick our way up Oak Creek Canyon as it cut through the Mogollon escarpment. Mike, who was riding in Jim Harper's van at the time, had been leap frogging up the highway to photographic vantage points where Jim would shoot stills and John would record videos as we passed by. Richie had suggested he do this to give me a roadside cheering section. Mike also wanted to be there because of his concern that the team had put too much of the hard part of this section of the course on Dina and my shoulders.

He was ahead of us on higher ground up the Canyon and had a cell phone connection with the RV waiting in Flagstaff. The Crew Chief, Joe Knopinski, was in the RV at the time, had tried to reach Bill to get an idea on our progress, but couldn't get through and had called Mike.

"Mike?" he asked. "Do you know where the girls are?"

"They're about 6 or 7 miles behind us." He answered.

"How are they doing? How's Amy doing?" Our problems with the heat, especially mine, had to have been a topic of discussion. There clearly was recognition of the work load we were undertaking out in the heat that day.

"Well, you've put them on the hardest climb, the longest segment on the hottest day so far; I'm concerned about Amy. She is the oldest, after all", Mike told Joe.

"I think you need to even out time on the bike", he added.

Mike still felt there hadn't been an adequate discussion when he brought up the four hour segment regimen adopted by other teams. Nor was there any conversation about alternatives or under what circumstances should pre-determined meeting points be changed.

"Take it easy, Mike. Look, we'll talk here about what our options might be", Joe went on, "and I'll call you back." And he hung up.

A few minutes later, he called again.

"Mike"

"Yeah," Mike responded.

"I think we have a plan. We're going to take Ann and Julie back down the highway to the top of the Switchbacks, which will cut off about 18 miles of their ride."

While this conversation was going on, down below, we had passed through Slide Rock Park which was 4 miles past Sedona. At this point, the canyon narrows, the road sides are shielded with namesake oaks and ponderosa pine. It was now after 5 pm and the sun was dropping below the rim of the canyon. And with increased elevation, the ambient air temperature declined as well.

When we were out in the open under the sun, each ride was progressively stressful as my body fought to lower my core temperature. But now, we were no longer directly in the sun. It wasn't pressing down on me as it had been before. The leafy canopy of the canyon provided protection. It was cooler. My body temperature didn't begin to spike during my segments as I rode through this shaded environment. I was being visually and atmospherically soothed. I began to feel better as the headache and nausea dissipated. My mood and my self- confidence improved and I remained strong during the course of each pull. I now got into an even climbing tempo, and began to take in the scenery around me.

I was back! I had made it through the "death zone" and I was still on the bike.

What a relief. I turned what had been a struggle into a triumph. To recover while still riding was a wonderful reinforcement that my conditioning wasn't an issue. I had beaten the fear of failure elephant back into the corner. As we gained elevation and the sun disappeared, the temperature kept declining in our favor.

I finished a turn several miles below the Sterling Springs switchbacks and had pulled up alongside Dina.

"Go Dina, We've got this one." I yelled.

"All right Amy!" she replied and pedaled up the road. She must have experienced the cooling effect too.

Paul came out and grabbed my bike to throw it on the rear rack of the Audi. I slid into the back seat, put my helmet in the accessories box and pulled out my food bag. Paul jumped in and we were off. I pulled a cold wash cloth out of my cooler and pressed it to my face.

After a minute we had caught up to Dina and the flashing lights of the Toyota and passed her.

Richie was driving and looked back at me over his shoulder.

"How's it going Amy?" he asked. "Is the heat still bothering you?"

"I'm good. It's all good," I responded.

"I got a call that there is a new plan to help you two out." he continued. "Joe says that they can cut off a part of your ride by driving Ann back to the top of the canyon where she and Julie can take it to the Flagstaff time station."

I could see Richie look at me in the rear view mirror as he talked. There was that instant where I visualized the physical release of being off the bike sprawled out on a bed in the back of the RV. Then I thought of the first time I met Ann and Julie. They had complained about the inability of one of the riders of their Race Across the West team to finish. They had repeated the story several times, which seemed to emphasize to me that reliability was going to be a critical ingredient for all the members of the team. This was something that I wanted very much to deliver. After that meeting, I had resolved that I was not going to be the subject of a dismissive appraisal at the end of RAAM if I could help it.

I listened and finished chewing a handful of potato chips. I thought – they're going to take over at the top of the canyon where the remaining ride is flat?

"No fucking way." I said. "I can finish my ride. No one's going to take it away from me now!"

"Yeah, well, Joe thought that you might need a longer recovery from your time in the heat." He continued.

"We're in the shade now, the temperature has dropped. It's not necessary. Call him back and tell him to forget it."

This information was relayed to Joe and our "rescue' was aborted although the belief that we (or I) needed such remained.

As I cranked up the last section of the Sterling Springs switchbacks, a point at which the grade became more moderate, it became even clearer to me that I had made it and I could feel this elation swelling inside me. Up ahead, I could make out Dina waiting in the headlights of the Toyota.

As I approached her for the exchange, she turned forward, pushed off and gathered speed; and as I drew alongside she shouted out "Yahoo!" as she pedaled into the gathering dusk.

We went back to longer pulls of 4 miles at a time as we finished our segment into Flagstaff. We reached the time station where the RV had stopped after 5 hours and 54 minutes of riding at an average speed of 16.1 mph – not bad considering. The Raw Milk Cats, doing 4 hours on, 4 hours off, had finished that section in 5:10 hrs. We were now 4:17 behind them.

15

When I came into the service area next to the RV, Dina was still finishing the last mile of our leg. The NBC TV crew was there and as I opened the car door, the producer Aarne Heikkila, pushed the camera at me.

"Amy, tell us what you think about the race now?" he asked.

I looked back at him and at the camera and thought about the last 95 miles we had just done.

"It's good," I said. "I'm hooked! What an adventure." I felt a great sense of relief and accomplishment wash over me and a smile spread across my face.

As I got out of the Audi, I saw Dina finish and Julie start as she took off on the next leg. Dina stopped and got off her bike as her brother, John took it from her to store on the back of the RV. We walked toward one another and instinctively grabbed each other and hugged. This sharing of adversity with Dina translated itself to a need to celebrate with an embrace. The TV crew was there and captured it. It made the 6 o'clock news.

After the TV crew had taken a few more shots and some further interview responses, we retreated to the RV. I squeezed into the bathroom and did a quick wash cloth clean up, changed out of my jersey and shorts into a comfortable short cotton skirt and t-shirt. Refreshed, I squeezed into the banquette beside Dina. Someone put a chicken and rice dish in front of me which I knew I had to eat. Shortly, Mike joined us. He had pulled my bike off the Audi and stored it on the back of the RV with Dina's. He slid his arm over my shoulder and gave me a quick hug.

"Nice going'", he said.

"Thanks", I replied.

We didn't talk much about the ride, but his just sitting there made a world of difference. He was my "soul" support crew. This became a ritual with us. He was my bike caddy, made sure I had all the food, ice and water I would need while riding and was there at the end of each ride, sustaining the belief I had in myself. It didn't seem like much. But it was.

So much of the 24 hour day was taken up with getting organized before each ride, eating, riding, finishing the ride, changing clothes and then trying to sleep in a bouncing RV only to repeat it all in 3 or 4 hours. It gave only small amounts of time for personal interaction with your relay partner, the other relay team and anyone else not in the car with you as your support crew. And even then, support crews were often distracted and sometimes distant. So sitting next to Mike for a couple minutes was my luxury.

Before we closed up the RV and started toward the next vehicle meeting point, Joe joined us and told us that a decision was made to extend Julie and Ann's next segment by 22 miles to a total of 94.4 miles, which would give us another hour of sleep. No complaints from Dina or me on that decision.

In my view, it would begin to even out the load. They would ride almost as far as we had just ridden, in the cool of the evening, starting with a 3,000 foot descent over the first half of the leg and from there only a 1,000 foot gradual climb over the remaining 45 miles along the southern edge of Monument Valley ending in Tonalea. They were pretty fresh and accomplished this in 4:57 hours, a speed just under 20 mph. It would be the first time LS&G had eclipsed the rate of speed between Time Stations recorded by RMC.

We would now be on Navajo Tribal lands, an area of sweeping vistas, and a landscape of red buttes and sage brush in the middle of the Painted Desert. I wouldn't see any of it. It would be at night. I would be in the back of the RV being bounced skyward as the rear wheels hit each crack in the road on our journey to the next meeting point.

In our quest to raise money for the race, we sold Time Stations to contributors and as we passed each one, the purchaser of that location was to be called by one of the support crew to let them know it had been reached. This was done most of the time, although as the race wore on, I'm sure some calls were missed. We were also trying to blog and add updates and pictures to our personal and team Facebook pages to give those following us a running narrative of our progress. It subsequently came to pass that a blurb was posted on the LS&G Facebook page that said,

"Amy and Dina struggled in the heat yesterday. Ann and Julie rode all but 2 ½ hours through the night to give them recovery. They are back on the road and all is well with LS&G!"

There is no question that we had had a tough day, and that getting an extra hour of recovery time was wonderful, but we did clock 16 mph despite the heat and the climbing. We had ridden all day from 5:11 am in the morning to 7:24 in the evening with a similarly short recovery period – 3 hours 2 minutes versus the 2 hours 42 minutes that Julie and Ann would end up with that evening. Yet despite the easier assignment they ended up with, I wouldn't have traded it for the satisfaction Dina and I took from fighting through the heat and finishing the climbs. It's RAAM after all. The world's toughest cycling endurance race. This day would go down as one of the high points of the race.

By the time we reached Tonalea, the team was 36 hours and 627 miles into the race. Dina and I had ridden for almost 20 hours and 330 of those miles and had completed 24,000 out of 36,000 feet of elevation gain and of those, 13,700 feet out of a total of 20,000 feet of the steeper grades. We were the workhorses of the race so far and I felt a wonderful pride in my accomplishments.

Importantly, I had felt no lingering effects from the heat. When you read the accounts of other RAAM racers or see videos of their experiences, you realize that throughout the race the line between a successful ride and abandonment can be thin. Not only is the heat in the "death zone" an obstacle, but it can be compounded by other problems. A minor muscle or ligament problem, a stomach issue or a small saddle sore can morph into something significantly more painful and serious, which would hinder or even put an end to one's race efforts.

During Shannon's RAAM, he had been given a food and liquid intake regimen from Carmichael Training Centers, yet succumbed to the heat. One of his team mates had ridden into a parallel joint between concrete pavement slabs and crashed. He rode with pain through the rest of the race with a large hematoma on his thigh. And closer to home, six weeks before we left for Oceanside, Mike crashed. He hit a chunk of cement in the road, twisting his front wheel which threw him over the handlebars. With no helmet on, he opened a scalp wound that needed 16 staples to close.

How far was I from hitting a crack in the road in the construction zone that I rode through and how close was I to having my core temperature go up another degree or two and encountering a problem not unlike Shannon's? I had been near the edge but hadn't cracked. But the real race doesn't start until Durango. That's when the lack of sleep begins to magnify the things that go wrong. What other issues would need to be overcome in scaling the Rockies, pushing across the windswept flats of Kansas and sweltering in the humid conditions of the Mississippi Valley?

Chapter 2

Beginnings

As the RV trundled toward Tonalea, my body was still tense from the physical and emotional stress of the last 14 hours. I tried to get some sleep, but the bouncing RV wouldn't let me. Dina was on one side of the queen size bed and I could feel her presence. Not being able to nod off to dreamland brought a new wave of worry. What if we faced another day like the one I just went through and I didn't get any sleep? How would I be able to hold up under those circumstances? Does this performance angst not go away? It was a little bit before 10 pm when the RV pulled to a stop at our next turn over location allowing me to finally drift off.

When I woke up, it was nearly midnight. It would shortly be Monday, June 18th; fifteen months from when I first heard about a chance to do RAAM. Fifteen months of training, racing, fund raising and planning; while continuing to sell real estate at Perry & Company. Fifteen months to the day when I received a phone call from Rainey Wikstrom, my old triathlon coach, asking me if I would be interested in being part of a 4 woman relay team.

Apparently, the team stumbled in its early organizational efforts. It had initially been comprised of four riders, who had done the

Race Across the West together in 2010, two as racers and two as crew members of which Rainey was one. The person who dropped out, had been the crew chief for that race, and did so because of a confrontation with Rainey. This was probably not a good sign had I been aware of it, but I wasn't at the time. I was just floored with the idea of doing a race that was so monumental.

My history with Rainey goes back to a year after I started racing the bike. I had been a competitive swimmer and life guard when I was young, a recreational and sometime competitive runner in recent years and now that I had a good bike, triathlons seemed like a natural step. I had been recommended to her by Celeste Callahan, who got women with no athletic background involved in competing in triathlons, but thought I was too advanced for her group. Celeste already had RAAM on her resume and Rainey was taken with the idea of doing it too. She brought it up a couple of times that summer and in response, I expressed an interest.

I ended up having a great year with her, finishing second in my age group in the Lake to Lake Olympic distance triathlon in Fort Collins and competed in a number of duathlons, that involve just running and biking, with decent results. The experience was such a positive one that I took pains to post comments on her website praising her coaching skills. But after my initial plunge into the sport, recurring problems with plantar fasciitis made me re-concentrate on cycling and other less joint impacting sports like rowing.

During the call, I agreed to meet that next day with her and the remaining two members for coffee. We were to gather at a Whole Foods market in South Denver. Unfortunately, in my haste to get there, I left the directions at home and went to the wrong store. When I didn't find them, I realized the mistake I had made. It was at a store a half dozen miles away in Littleton. Now I was going to be late.

As I pulled out of the parking area to go to the correct location my phone rang. It was Rainey.

"Well are you coming?' she asked with annoyance in her voice.

"Of course, I am", I answered and explained my mistake.

The two other team members were Ann Lantz and Julie Lyons. They had been the riders on the 2010 RAW team on which Rainey had crewed. Ann was then 48, a Personal Trainer and led early morning spinning classes, while Julie was 55, had been trained as a nurse, but had left that career to raise a family and coach young triathletes. Both had been designated All American Age-Group Triathletes with a long list of successes including competing in the sport for the U.S. in World Masters events.

Ann was lean and of moderate height with bangs of light reddish hair down to her eyebrows. Her hair was pulled back in a ponytail. She was bubbly, very verbal and chatty and tended to repeat a lot of what was said by others.

Julie was shorter, maybe a little over 5 feet tall, but she looked solidly built. She had curly dark hair which was beginning to show some grey, a long oval face and was more serious in her conversation, although she had a habit of following each of her points with a forced laugh, as if she sensed a need to soften or deprecate what she had just said.

Rainey appeared to be the driving force behind the RAAM effort and was enthusiastic and positive about the team's prospects, while Julie and Ann were initially a little more reticent. After our "get acquainted" conversation, Rainey got right to the point. She wanted to know if I would join their team. And in all honesty, I wanted to say yes. But signing up for this race was going to be a huge commitment. I wanted to digest what it all implied and to mull over the impact it would have on my daily schedule and my lifestyle.

So I told her again, "This is a big decision for me. My job is pretty demanding and I'd like to talk to Mike about it. Let me think about it over the weekend."

This seemed not to be adequate and she asked again, "Okay, but do you think you'll do it?"

So in response I asked, "Well, tell me where you stand organizationally and with raising money and what are the demands on me and importantly, what do you think it's going to cost?"

There weren't a lot of hard answers forthcoming. The team organization was still in its infancy. I got the impression that it was going to cost as much as $10,000 per rider. They had identified one of their support crew from RAW, Joe Knopinski, who had agreed to be Crew Chief and had names of several other crew volunteers, but were still a long way from having a full complement on board.

At least they had a charity. Rainey had suggested one which would accept donations for our team and fund our race expenses, while keeping a portion for their programs. This made all donations we received tax deductible.

The charity was LiveWell Colorado, which had a hand in Rainey's day job as a Wellness Consultant to a local Adams County school. LiveWell's mission is to combat childhood obesity through better diet and active living and had developed programs to train school cafeteria staff, locate local sources of farm fresh foods, created activity curriculum for students and similar school and community directed initiatives and had been instrumental on the establishment of a state level school nutrition body. This was a worthwhile cause, although it had limitations on attracting donations from people living outside the state.

There was also a fund raising affair on the books. Rainey had organized a wine tasting, which would be the first major event. Julie and Ann were just getting started with their efforts although Ann was leading Friday afternoon rides for $5 a head and had thrown a party to raise funds for upgrading her bicycle.

Another point was that team members would train independently and would be responsible for putting in the necessary hours to attain a high level of fitness. We needed to develop our own training regimen and stick with it. Ann, in addition to the charity rides, ran an early morning spin class. She appeared fit and I didn't think she would have an issue with training. Julie also looked in good shape, and for her small size, she looked to have good power. Moreover, she was in the process for training for a World Masters Triathlon event in Beijing that summer.

As for Rainey, her level of fitness probably wasn't there yet. She was a tall, broad shouldered woman with attractive Nordic features, as her name might suggest. But, she was big. Her triathlon successes were in the Athena Division, that's for women over 150 lbs. And to my eye, Rainey's weight was a few ticks past that.

When the conversation got around to the 2010 RAW experience, I was given a description of the relay plan. There would be 2 sets of partners pairing up. Only one rider would be on the road at a time and would change off with her partner in a relay format every 20 minutes or so. Beyond that, there wasn't much detail and I was still vague about the specifics. Other information about equipment needs, sleep deprivation, food intake, weather or other race-centric issues didn't command much discussion.

But they did talk about the physical demands on riders and how they could break down. During RAW two of their teammates had reached points at which they couldn't or wouldn't get back on the bike. Julie's partner ran out of gas when they were 80 miles from the finish in Durango and was described as "laying down in the road and refusing to ride anymore". On another occasion, Ann ended up doing an extended solo climb when her relay partner stopped riding. Apparently, her partner's navigator failed to recognize a turn on the road causing an off course ride of some distance in the wrong direction. This upset her to the point that she begged off riding for a while.

They repeated these stories several times during that first meeting. While their team ended up setting a RAW record for women's 4 person relay teams over 2 days of non-stop racing, the issues experienced with their 2 partners were the only ones worth emphasizing. I became uncomfortable with the thought that I might reach a point where I could not get on the bike; and that I would be the subject of the same failure. On the other hand, it did leave a strong message that I needed to make a commitment to do the training that was required. Ann and Julie clearly didn't want someone else on the team who would end up lying in the road; and I certainly didn't want to be remembered that way. I had confidence in myself. I thought I had the kind of mental and physical constitution that would carry me through, but the fear of failure was nevertheless imprinted.

As I soaked it all in, I could feel those butterflies in my stomach when I thought about the thrill of the challenge, the risks, the adventure and the enormity of the event. It was so enticing. But, again I told them that I would have to think about it and discuss it with Mike before reaching a decision.

And I did have real concerns. First, Rainey didn't appear to be fit. Although she had enough time to get in shape, it wasn't a good place to start. Second, she had repeatedly dwelled on the necessity to raise funds as well as asking me with some urgency, if I was interested on joining the team. My reaction to her line of conversation was that she was worried about not raising enough money, and wanted me to join because she considered me a good source for my share. It occurred to me that while they said they were talking to candidates, I was the only live body they had at the time. And finally, in reality, it was really hard to wrap my arms around what a race of this magnitude would be like and how the preparation would affect my life. So I just needed to think about it.

But before I left, Rainy looked at me anxiously one last time and asked yet again, "you're going to do it, aren't you?"

When I got home, I broached the story to Mike. There was excitement in my voice, but I felt a little guilty about the fact he would not be involved in the competition. After all, except for doing triathlons and the odd yoga class, we did most all of our training and races together. And he was the guy that got me into all of this in the first place. So I first suggested – weakly – that maybe we could do the Race Across the West, together as a 2 person team.

"...or maybe we could..." I searched for a connection.

"Come on Amy," he smiled. "You've got to be kidding. You have to do this. This is you're moment, a great, once in a lifetime, opportunity."

At this point in my business life, I had built up a very good real estate career. I was proud of what I had accomplished and wanted to sustain it. But the real estate market was recovering slowly due to the after effects of the recession, meaning, on the one hand, I had time to train, but on the other, needed to work harder to generate activity. Moreover, the race occurred in June at a time when residential real estate activity was usually pretty high. So I had to get my mind around that.

Mike had no hesitation. He was in complete acceptance of the whole thing.

"Do it," he said more than once.

When I asked questions about fund raising, what our out of pocket costs would end up being, equipment requirements or my business over the summer, his response was, "we'll figure it out", or "that shouldn't be a problem".

In the end this is what I wanted him to say. I was getting to a point in my life when I wouldn't be able to contemplate doing something like this anymore. I needed to grab it before it was gone. And the more I internalized it, the more comfortable I became about doing RAAM.

Still, I wanted the weekend to think about it. Rainey, still anxious for a decision, called on Saturday afternoon to see if I had decided and I had to fend her off again. But I called her as promised on Monday morning from my office.

Her phone only rang once before she answered' "Hello."

"Hi Rainey, its Amy. I'm in", I said.

Chapter 3

The Program

Just as it had with training for a triathlon, I knew that engaging a coach to put a specific training program together, monitor my results, and offer an outside source of support and validation, would give me the structure and discipline that I would need.

And I knew who I was going to pick as a trainer. Immediately upon putting the telephone down after telling Rainey I was in, I picked it back up and called Kathy Zawadski. Kathy and her husband John ran Peak to Peak Training Systems which offered a range of programs for competitive cyclists. I was introduced to Kathy by, a good friend and rowing partner, Nomi Notman, who had trained to race bicycles with her and was a big fan.

During the past two winters, Mike and I had often gone to their indoor facilities for work out sessions on their CompuTrainers™. Most serious cyclists own a bicycle trainer for stationary riding. This is a contraption that raises the rear wheel off the ground and clamps it against a rotor that provides resistance. CompuTrainers™ add a monitor and control electronics that tie together a video of an actual race and its physical profile, so that as the course climbs and descends, the resistance from the training device changes correspondingly to simulate race conditions. It also gives riders a constant feedback on heart rate, wattage output, pedaling efficiency, distance and speed. It was a welcome change from grinding away on a stationary trainer in the basement during the winter with no feedback.

Kathy and I agreed to meet for coffee the next day. She had not worked with RAAM competitors before and wanted to know all about the race and the riding demands for relay team members. After I explained the routine, she shook her head, yes, that she understood and began to talk in general terms about what I could expect.

"Volume, Amy, volume," she concluded.

"And Amy, you can't cheat. Don't skip workouts. You won't make it across the country if you do," she added.

When she said this, that image of lying on the road somewhere in West Virginia crept into my mind. I didn't want to shortchange myself. I wanted to assure my success. After meeting with Kathy, I took the rest of the afternoon off, went home, jumped on the bike and took a 2 hour ride.

The first workout downloads came on May 13, 2011. It would be another year and a month, a total of 57 weeks or 399 days before the June 16th start of the 2012 RAAM. I would receive an email every day with a workout plan and what was on the plate for the following day. These workouts could change or be switched depending on what I had completed. It wasn't all cycling. I planned to row at the U.S. Masters National Regatta in Oklahoma City in July and at the FISA International Masters Regatta in Poznan, Poland, in September, which meant there would be indoor and outdoor rowing sessions on my schedule. There was yoga and some weight lifting as well. But every day, my download was there. It became a big elephant in the room.

Each proposed workout was listed with a neutral gray background. As I downloaded my daily results from a Garmin 500 that recorded my ride by time, distance, speed, pedal cadence and heart rate, it would change color. If I hit the minimum time required, it would turn a reassuring green. If I missed, it turned an angry, disapproving red. If I hand entered something, like a yoga workout, it changed to yellow. Yellows were acceptable, but green was the most soothing. Reds engendered anxiety.

The schedule of a residential real estate broker is not terribly consistent. Sometimes in the winter months activity is slow. In the summer, it can be hectic. It is often necessary to be available when clients have time; meaning evenings and weekends can be busy. Deliberating an offer or a counter proposal can sometimes drag on into the night. As a consequence, it requires me to be flexible. Furthermore, I like to spend a reasonably full day at the office to stay in the flow of things. That meant planning for the necessary time for the "volume", Kathy promised in her workout routine would require discipline on my part.

Fortunately, Denver is a city that encourages cycling. It's also a sport you can do from your front door. We live near streets that have designated bike lanes and are not far from Washington Park and City Park that offer roads with limited vehicular traffic. Then, there are miles and miles of major bike trails that run along Cherry Creek, Sand Creek, Clear Creek and the Platte River, the closest of which is only 4 blocks away. Getting in a 30 to 40 mile ride without putting your foot down a whole bunch of times is relatively easy to accomplish.

That first day, a Friday, called for Core 101, a series of exercises from the www.coreperformance.com website. This included 4 x 1 minute repetitions of forward, right side and left side planks, 8 to 15 repetitions of some gluteus bridging exercises and several crunch moves. Strengthening core and gluteus muscles would pay dividends when spending hours in the saddle for 7 days in a row. But, I rode my bike for an hour and a half instead. I was usually on target for cycling workouts, and if I was weak in following the schedule for anything, it was with these core sessions. I rationalized these choices in the belief that the amount of time I spent rowing would compensate. I believed, or perhaps a better word was "hoped" that this would not come back to haunt me during the race.

For the next year, I would begin the day by logging into my computer to look for any messages that came in during the night. I subscribed to an online data provider that automatically sent out new Multiple Listing Service entries. I could program the requests to meet specific client search requirements. Each night these would be sent out, and the next morning, I might get an email from a client requesting a showing. In addition, during busy periods there was always traffic regarding offers, closing instructions, loan commitment letters, extensions, inspections, and you name it. Now, I got to add another step. It was to look at my scheduled workout. Then after looking at what was already on my calendar for the day, I would begin to piece together how I was going fit everything in. Some days, I had plenty of time and on other days, not so much. I might switch a long training day for yoga in the afternoon or an early morning row or, and let's be honest here, take the day off. But, by the end of each week, for the most part, I got my volume.

The first full week called for 12 hours of total training time. I put in 13:32 hours. This included an hour of rowing, a half hour warm up for a mid-week race that was cancelled because of thunderstorms, 4 and a half hours of riding with a high cadence and low intensity on Saturday and almost 3 hours of rolling hills on Sunday. Some of the riding was from the house, but there could be an hour or more each day of travel time when we opted to vary the scenery by going outside of Denver to ride. Also, there was time involved in getting dressed, filling water bottles and the like. Fortunately for me, Mike, took care of maintaining my bikes, although an occasional trip down to my bike shop, Turin Bikes, was sometimes necessary.

Plus, I had a training partner. Mike would be with me. He would plan our routes based on the specifics of the workout, and the time and intensity required. He was also out front setting a pace for me to follow most of the time. Although some early morning rides, I did alone. Each evening, I would look at Kathy's workout plan for the next 2 days and then look at my business calendar. If I saw a logjam, I would get up for an early ride down the South Platte trail to the Chatfield Reservoir and back. When I did these rides, more often than not, Mike would pull the pillow over his head and mumble something about, "having breakfast ready", when I got back. Early morning has never proven to be the best part of his day.

By the time I got to Oceanside to begin the race, I had 15 months of training under my belt, and in the year before the race started, the data gathered by my Garmin totaled 572 hours and 28 minutes of workout time on the bike, with distance covered of 5,444 miles. This included time spent on indoor training rides for which no miles are recorded and rowing workouts in my single shell, during which distance covered was significantly less than would be on a bike. I had completed another 21 hours of core strengthening exercises and yoga.

I also got in some rowing miles. Because of the regattas I planned to row that summer, I continued training on the water. While I mounted my Garmin to pick up workouts in my single shell, I didn't gather data for practices in boats in which I trained and raced with other rowers. But I think the total I spent on training and racing added another 30 hours or so. For me this was a very modest commitment to rowing compared to prior years and while my legs were strong from cycling, I was less fit as far as arm strength is concerned.

Nevertheless, in August at the Oklahoma City Nationals, I brought home a Silver Medal in the 60-64 years of age mixed double sculls event that I rowed with one of Mike's teammates and a Bronze in a women's 55-59 quad. Mike and I made it to the finals in a 65-69 age mixed double, but finished out of the medals.

I also won Gold as a cox in a Men's Club eight that Mike stroked, although coxing is not something I feel is my strength. While I'm the right size for a coxswain, my competitive nature gets the best of me and I tend to get emotional during the race, particularly when it's close. Typically, to get a boat to go faster, the stroke rate needs to be higher, and barring a loss of cohesion and efficiency amongst the crew, this will work. However, sustaining a higher stroke rate can lead to a depletion of oxygen and energy stores in the muscles. Nevertheless, given my excitability, I like to call the stroke rate up.

While a cox sits directly in front of the rower in the stroke seat, she (or he) tends to look past him (or her) down the course so as to steer a straight line, to watch the timing of the crew's oars, and to monitor the other boats in the race, if there are any ahead. Had I looked at Mike in the stroke seat in Oklahoma City that day when we entered the last 250 meters, I would have seen the pained, urgent and somewhat desperate look on Mike's face as I yelled in my microphone "Take it up....Up two...NOW!" There was a boat in the next lane challenging us, maybe 2 or 3 seats down and I wanted to open some space. But, the stroke rate was already high and the crew behind him was rushing the slide which limits the boat's run. He was already at his limit and if anything, wanted the rate down to eliminate the rush. He tried, but taking the stroke rate up was not an option. There would be no 2 strokes up for him, despite my insistence. That'll teach him to make me the cox.

In early September, we traveled to Poznan, Poland to row at FISA. FISA is the organization that oversees world rowing competitions and these events are held 3 out of every 4 years in Europe, drawing over 3,000 competitors each time. Mike and I have competed at a dozen of these annual regattas since I first started to row 16 years ago. It's taken us to countries and regions that we wouldn't have thought of going to otherwise and we have had many great experiences. Mike is part of a collection of men his age from the U.S. who regularly go to these events. I used to put together a group of top American women under the Denver Boat Club to row in these events, but now compete with the Master's International Women's team. Rowers in this group are successful veteran athletes from a number of European countries principally Germany and France as well as the U.S.

In Poznan, I had a very successful regatta, winning a gold medal in the women's 60-64 eight oared shell and in a similarly aged four oared shell with cox, which I stroked. I also won as the bow of a quadruple scull race.

But my best race was in a double scull in the 60-64 age group with Jill Gardner, a terrific American rower. She and I would be racing against Merete Boldt, a dominant Dutch sculler and perennial gold medalist and her British partner. It was a barn burner of a race. At the start, after a couple of short quick strokes to get moving, we took the rating up and began a sprint. We got a good jump initially, but after a few strokes of the sprint, I could see we were steering to port, which tracked us toward the lane buoys on that side of the course. If your oar blades go across the buoy line, they can get hung up in the ropes and make the catch and release difficult. As we began to hit buoys, I yelled "PORT, PORT OAR!!" to get Jill to pull hard with me on the port side to correct our heading.

Gradually, we straightened, and despite our early problem, opened up a slight lead. We held it as we went through the halfway mark in first; 3 seconds ahead of a boat from Hungary. I don't know what problems Merete had at the start, but she came through halfway in 4th place out of 7 boats, not typical for her. But from there, she and her partner dropped the hammer.

We had spent a lot of energy on a high cadence start and then on struggling with the buoys. They were in the lane next to us and on each of the 60 strokes remaining; we could see them eat a half a foot or more into our lead. They moved through a German crew, and then the Hungarians who were dying at that point and began to eat into the two boat lengths between us. They were flying when we hit 100 meters to go. They had edged to a half a boat length down and were out-stroking us. I could feel lactic acid build in my lats, arms and shoulders and then in my legs, but true to form, I called the rating up for the last ten strokes and we threw it all out there. Sucking in big gulps of air, we drove to the finish, pulling away with the last 3 or 4 strokes.

The finishing horn beeped, and then again, 1.8 seconds later it sounded for Merete, and then successively for the other 5 boats as they went across the line. I slumped in exhaustion. My heart was racing, my chest was still heaving and I bent over the oars exhausted. Oh, but what a wonderful feeling. I had won a fourth Gold medal.

These races are only 1,000 meters in length, and after a 20 minute warm-up, they take around 4 minutes to finish. It is not the most compatible cross training discipline for an endurance cycling event, but it certainly didn't hurt and was a great diversion to training on the bike.

Fortunately, we did get a lot of cycling in during our trip. While we were in Poznan, we stayed in the reconstructed old town in a place called the Brovaria, which was a small hotel above a brewpub on the Stare Miasto, a large cobblestone square lined with beer tents. We rented hybrid bikes to use on the daily five mile trip to the race course, and to explore the city when we weren't racing.

We spent several days in Berlin, which is a great bike friendly city. Our hotel, which was near Checkpoint Charlie, had cruiser bikes available, which made it easy to tour the city. After that we ended up spending a week cycling on high end Cannondale carbon road bikes in and around Cahors and the Dordogne region of France. This is the contested area of the Hundred Years War when the English tried to exercise their claim on the French throne and the French weren't able to kick them out until Joan of Arc got them organized. The whole thing just needed a woman's resolve.

Here, we rode an average of 40 miles each day, enjoying excursions to some of the tourist destinations like the medieval villages of Sarlat and Brantome, and to cliffside medieval castles overlooking serpentine rivers at St. Cirq la Popie and Rocamador, up and down narrow country roads, stopping at an occasional sign reading 'Dégustation' that announced a vineyard offering tastes and sales of its wines. These weren't the fee based, commercial enterprises that one encounters in the U.S., but simple farm buildings where the farmer proudly offers tastes of his product. Sight-seeing by bicycle was an enjoyable way to see the countryside, add to my training volume and offer a defensive offset to the heavy, rich menus that was the standard fare in the region.

Adding in an estimate for these rides, by the time I lined up in Oceanside, I had trained for 650 hours and covered in excess of 6,000 miles on the bike. I also rowed a total of 70 miles or so, which corresponds to roughly 500 miles of cycling. Reading the stories of RAAM solo riders, this was about half of what some of them undertake during their training. Making sure I satisfied the need for an adequate amount of time training would always be a concern.

But while I needed to devote more hours to training than I typically did, I still led a normal life. I was able to devote a comprehensive effort to my real estate career and sustained a very good level of business throughout this period. In 2012, for the tenth time, I was named to the Denver Realtor's Roundtable of Excellence for top producers.

This commitment to training did not require the adoption of a monastic existence or a rigid diet. I was able to enjoy a good glass of wine with my dinner and a cold beer on a hot day. My social life was as busy as before. I was able to spend time gardening. What I concluded from my experience is that this type of effort, seemingly epic in most people's minds, is an achievable objective for a much broader segment of the population than might be thought. It is a reachable goal for many of those who consider it not to be.

Chapter 4

Money and Mucho Gusto

After my acceptance, the four of us began to meet once every couple of weeks or get together on a conference call. The topic of these early meetings was fund raising. Julie had come up with a $38,000 estimate of what it would cost to participate in the race. This was an extrapolation of the expenses that the RAW team had incurred. We would have to pay for racers and crew to get to Oceanside and back from Annapolis, lodging at both ends, meals, food during the race, the rental of 2 mini-vans and a big RV plus gas, communication and navigation electronics, spare bike parts, and so on.

The race is a significant financial obligation; which was yet another big elephant in the room. Raising the money necessary to do this was going to be a challenge.

This would add to the other two elephants that I had to deal with. The first one was Fear of Failure. He usually hid in the corner and wasn't bothersome except every once in a while, late at night, when I couldn't get to sleep, he would come out and keep me company. That one wouldn't completely go away until the race ended, unless I quit, which wasn't likely. The second one was Training and Work Schedule. A couple of back to back red days on my web page would increase his presence. That one would hopefully go away when we left for Oceanside. But now, added to the mix, was the Fund Raising Elephant. It was a crowded room.

The first event on the agenda for raising money was the upcoming wine tasting. We tasked one another with getting contributions of items we could offer in a silent auction that would be going on during the event. I was able to tap into a list of in-kind donors for massages, training sessions and gift certificates, as were the others. But, I decided not to promote it to my friends. I planned to host my own event closer to the date of the race at a location near where I lived. My thinking was, I would get the greatest return through that approach. I told the other girls of this decision during a meeting and seemed to receive acceptance, although I was never completely sure.

We also worked on drafting a solicitation letter for sponsors, but this would not be a fund sources that would prove viable for us. Our team's ability to attract a major sponsor was not strong. Everyone chases after the bike manufacturers and component suppliers such as producers of bike wheels, tires and accessories like Garmin GPS devices. They are common targets for teams such as ours, but there needs to be a compelling story or an impressive list of team members to get their attention. What success we had was in generating contributions of in-kind items such as apparel, travel duffels, discounted bike accessories and auction items, but coming up with a major financial sponsor to brand our team was something we were unable to achieve.

Energy food producers were modest contributors. Generation UCAN provided drink mixes. I used a Shaklee mix provided by Dean Smith, one of their distributors. I also received donations of energy food and chews from Honey Stinger products of Steamboat Springs, along with 6 cases of Mix One protein drink from the Boulder based company of that name. It was a brand owned by The Hershey Co. that folded not long after our race when 16,000 cases of product were found to be contaminated with mold and yeast. It was probably a good thing it wasn't a popular drink with our team during the race.

However, there was one source of corporate sponsorship that was available. Two of the Denver area Audi dealers provided vehicles for cycling teams that year. In fact, the manager of one of the Audi dealer's where I had my car serviced in Lakewood heard I was doing RAAM, and asked if we were looking for support. I said yes, but with the race so far in the future, I failed to follow up in a timely manner to nail him down. His dealership ended up giving 3 SUV's to several local cycling teams including a spacious Q7, that were completely wrapped with colorful promotional logos for the teams and the dealership. Obviously, they were looking for visibility around town. I learned a lesson that I should take on more urgency in these matters. Fortunately, a month or so before our race, Julie mentioned that she lived near the owner of MacDonald's Audi of Denver dealership. I encouraged her to ask them for support. She did and lo and behold, they extended the use of a Q5 for the race. That reduced our vehicle rental costs by one.

Over the following months, I tried to tap into what advice I could get from people who had been successful in raising money for rides. We met and had dinner with a business partner of Richie's father who had organized a ride for ex-Navy SEALS from California to New Orleans with the idea of raising money for combat wounded. His main source of funds came from a partner at Goldman Sachs. Another solo rider, who was the father-in-law of one of my associates at Perry & Company had done four distance rides raising over a half million dollars for 3 charities and was in the midst of trying to raise $1 million on a ride from Canada to Mexico down the coast. David Boyce, who was a friend of one of Mike's rowing partner's had a similar story. He had raised money for the Livestrong Foundation on two different rides, one coast to coast and the other down the Mississippi River from Canada to the Gulf.

The latter 2 were men a little older than me, who were retired. They took their time riding across the country, stopping at various towns to talk about their charities and their riding and fund raising objectives. What I gained from these meetings were several things. First, there was no silver bullet. Fund raising was going to take time and effort. Second, there needs to be a passion for one's charity. It makes the whole thing a lot easier when it's something that strikes you as important and helps to capture the emotions of the contributor. Thirdly, these men had great stories; really terrific experiences. They saw the country up close, enjoyed help and hospitality from strangers and got some healthy exercise. Their adventures were enviable.

Len Forkas, who was racing RAAM solo, was a great example of someone who had a cause he was passionate about. Mike met Len and his group at the Crew Seminar he attended earlier in the year. He was riding for HopeCam, a charity he helped found when his son contracted Leukemia and needed to be kept in isolation. Len arranged an open video feed linked to his son's classroom so he wouldn't lose his connection to his school and classmates. To date, HopeCam has raised money for nearly 300 home-bound kids in 6 countries to provide video connections to their schools.

It so happened that during one of our conference calls, Julie mentioned another Colorado based team that had completed RAAM several years before and had raised a quarter million dollars for the Denver Children's Hospital. She had the home phone number of Evan Zucker, who was the principal organizer of team Mucho Gusto. Evan was the managing principal of Black Creek Capital, a successful real estate investment firm in Denver. No one had contacted him up to that point, so I took it upon myself to do so in the hopes of gaining some insight.

I called and left a message that I was part of a team doing RAAM and I wanted to meet someone in the flesh who had completed it and learn about their fund raising approach and race experiences. A week later he called and apologized for not getting back sooner and agreed to meet me for coffee. It was a chilly spring morning when we met and the line for orders at Starbuck's was quite long. So despite the temperature, we decided to sit outside and talk.

While I wanted to hear how and from whom his team was able to generate the level of financial support they received, I also wanted to talk about doing the race. He told me that it had been his dream to do RAAM and as it turned out, he was the primary organizer and financial sponsor of the team. Evan had enlisted several friends to be on his support crew, recruited the other riders and hired a bunch of college kids from Colorado University to fill in the rest of his manpower needs. The team signed on with Chris Carmichael's Training Center in Colorado Springs, and received a comprehensive training program. This included individual testing to establish each rider's physiology, work capacity, caloric intake requirements and such. They were all experienced cyclists and one, George Hagerman was particularly adept as a climber.

Evan referred to the race as a great adventure, a word he used often, but for the team, the race was plagued with mishaps. Based on Evan's reminiscence that morning, and at a similar meeting I had a week later with Shannon Gillespie, I heard their RAAM story. Evan also shared with me a DVD by Altitude Sports, a Denver cable network, which captured their story for local broadcast.

It seemed to be a run of the mill RAAM experience until they hit the death zone in the section between Congress and Prescott, AZ, when things began to go badly. Starting at 9:00 am in the morning the sun was already sending down its powerful rays and the temperature would climb to 114°. Shannon began to run into difficulty during the 8 mile, 1,800 foot climb up the Yarnell Grade. It was here that the combination of heat and inadequate hydration would take its toll. His resulting heat stroke, loss of strength and inability to ride was just the beginning of the crises the team would encounter.

For the next 12 hours, they were down to 3 riders and when they got to Durango, pulled into a motel and crashed for a brief period of time. They did receive another short break when the organizers halted the race because of the accident that killed Bob Breedlove, a veteran endurance cyclist, who had done RAAM several times before. He had started several days ahead of the relay teams with other solo riders and had been hit by a pick-up truck in eastern Colorado. While they got a reprieve from cycling, the reason for it was emotionally unsettling.

When they got back on the road and headed up into the Rockies, their best climber, George, mistook towelettes from a Clorox disinfecting container for Wet-Wipes, to attend to his bottom. Not only did this cause immediate pain, it made sitting in the saddle unbearable. So on their ride out of Durango, they went from 3 to 2 riders to handle the Baldy Mountain and Wolf Creek Pass before Shannon was able to muster enough strength to take over on the long downhill toward Alamosa.

Then the hard crash and bruised hip sustained by one of the team was followed by a driver mutiny. The original bus driver asked to be replaced. He was used to high speed interstate driving of rock star bands and was going nuts puttering along secondary roads and stopping every 80 miles. The bus company had to fly in a replacement. The race is hard enough on its own, but dealing with these problems added an element of stress that made it even tougher.

At one point near the end of the race, the Altitude Sports film crew recorded George's rating of the race. "For seeing the country and for adventure, it's a TEN," he said, "but as far as being enjoyable, it's a ONE!"

Given that Evan was the source of money, this limited what I could gather about that part of the team development process. But as I listened to their recollections, I was enthralled. I should have been asking myself, what was I thinking of in agreeing to do this? But instead, I thought, these guys dealt with a lot of adversity, yet they made it. And to the extent I already had concerns; their story didn't make them any worse. In a perverse way, it made it more alluring, more of a challenge. Moreover, I believed that the bad luck Much Gusto encountered was unusual, although I did get the message on the need to eat and hydrated sufficiently - loud and clear. Once again, the idea of not being able to fully contribute was not how I saw myself. I didn't want to end up bonked on the side of the road. As for the bathroom, plain old toilet paper was going to be fine. But for fund raising, I was still looking for good advice.

If believing that I could train, complete RAAM and raise money for LiveWell and the race was measured on that same one to ten scale, my conviction meter was high. While I couldn't say it was a ten, it was at least a solid nine. But during my occasional nighttime sleeplessness, it wavered below that. To use a mixed metaphor, that's when the elephants entered the room.

Chapter 5

Branded

As for generating attention to our team, our charity, and our race objectives, there hadn't been a broad out-reach up to this point. The name that had been chosen was "Rocky Mountain RAAM". It seemed generic and non-specific and I thought we needed to come up with something a little snappier. Because of our sex, being of a certain age and the LiveWell charity, I thought we needed something that could identify us and create greater crowd appeal.

Mike's "Rocky Mountain RAAMettes" was a non-starter. We tried to come up with some other catchy names, but hadn't received a positive response from Julie and Ann.

Julie had created a website, but had not added a donation page. At one of our early meetings she mentioned that she was looking for ideas on creating a "donate" button to direct site visitors to the appropriate page. It occurred to me that, a client of mine Tasso Stathopoulos, had generated some wonderful art for his home, and his commercial credits included the award winning graphics and branding done for Noodles & Company, a national chain of restaurants based in Boulder. I thought he would be a great source for just such suggestions. And after our meeting, I gave him a call.

I told him about the racing team I had joined and all about RAAM; then explained our current situation. Could he give us any suggestions on our website and how to drive visitors to a donation page? I also thought, if he got interested in our team he might help us with graphics.

"What's the Team's name", he asked?

"Rocky Mountain RAAM", I replied.

"Oh", was the response. "Hmmmm let me think about it".

Several hours later I got a call back.

"John and I would like to meet with you and make some suggestions," he said.

"Tasso, that's wonderful", I replied, delighted that he had gotten back to me so quickly and that his creative partner, another real estate client of mine, John Bellina, was also interested in being involved.

We agreed that we would meet the following Friday morning at a Starbuck's in Cherry Creek.

I had asked for suggestion on graphics for a website donation page button and hoped it might turn into a broader level of support. But, I didn't have an inkling about what John and Tasso might be thinking about and whether they were interested in helping us beyond some initial brainstorming. My expectations were that they would ask me about the event and the team, and would in turn offer some suggestions of how we should proceed.

I turned out to be wrong. First of all, they were captured by the idea of the race and of the four women who intended to race it.

They bought into the excitement, the adventure and the appeal it could possibly have to others.

Secondly, they concluded that the team needed a branding campaign. John described the one they did for the Adams County library district which had received a National Medal of Excellence presented by Michelle Obama at the White House. Their firm, Ricochet Ideas, had created a campaign around the brand "Anythink" which attempted to expand the image of the library in the user's mind. It worked. Their efforts significantly increased library use in the community, an impressive feat in the era of the internet.

He then said, "What we would like to offer you is a branding campaign, pro bono. We've come up with the name Love Sweat & Gears for your team and we want to retain all naming and design rights and you have to accept our decisions."

Wow!

Tasso then pulled out several renderings to include the team name in an Edwardian Script with a red flame motif with a lace background and a stylized bicycle chain ring in the shape of a heart. It captured it all; the femininity, the drive and the passion. It was truly a gifted design. It was fantastic. It gave us an image to aspire to.

I was beside myself. First of all, this just removed a great deal of time we would need to devote to doing this on our own, so giving up control was an easy decision to make. And secondly, their suggestions were terrific, they were far and away better than anything the four of us could have conceived. John and Tasso would prove to be a valuable resource for us. What they were creating was something that our budget would not allow us to go into the market and acquire. Their retention of rights seemed an easy trade off.

Before we finished, I had promised to get the rest of the team together at the beginning of the following week to hear their presentation. Then I went home to worry. I was quite taken by the name they came up with, their logo design, the styling and their interest in providing us with a branding campaign. But at the same time, I was concerned with how the others would respond. Would they have the same reaction? Julie and Ann had been unresponsive to alternative names that I had offered before, would they react to "Love Sweat & Gears" the same way? Rainey had become increasingly tense and critical of my ideas during our fund raising update conferences; I suspected it was because of the glacial progress I was making on that front. But I worried it would spill over to this area as well.

With everyone juggling schedules, we finally met on Tuesday at my office. After introducing themselves, John and Tasso, interviewed us as to our motivations and ambitions as it related to RAAM. And then, began to describe a branding campaign designed to establish our image. This included the name and logo motif and a uniform design; and proceeded to talk about building the team's brand around a "warrior spirit" and linking it to active living and good health. There needed to be a strategy to develop a "movement" to embrace the broader theme of overcoming obstacles such as the one we were tackling in racing RAAM and the anti-obesity programs and objectives of LiveWell. Around the table, eyes widened, as it all soaked in. Any concerns I had that there would be resistance to their suggestions were misplaced. Julie, Ann and even Rainey were as taken as I was. So John and Tasso would be unleashed to work their magic.

In addition to our new name and logo, they created and produced for us to sell, several hundred promotional T-shirts featuring the heart shaped chain wheel with catchy sayings on the back. Tasso's design work would eventually include supplying design formats to Santini, an Italian cycling apparel company for short and long sleeve jerseys, jackets, vest and leg and arm warmers. He worked with Voler, a domestic company, to produce semi-custom practice jerseys, which we could get with a short delivery time. This would enable us to wear a jersey with our logo on it for promotional activities. The branding program eventually included crew shirts and hoodies, and LS&G logo buttons.

One of Tasso's prize creations was the heart shaped bicycle chain wheel necklace charm that Trice Jewelers made for us. Ann's husband worked in marketing at the firm and was able to work out an agreement where they would have the mold created and offer it for sale sharing some of the profits with the team. Initially, we received our own versions that included 5 small diamonds following the five bolt design of chain wheels, but the pendant that was offered to general public was a plain sterling silver design and was sold with a leather necklace. I did register a small coupe when one of my good friends and a client ordered a version with small rubies instead of diamonds. With the right promotion and advertising, we probably could have sold hundreds of them. But Trice retained control over production and marketing. Enough were sold to generate several thousand dollars for LiveWell and the team.

After the Ricochet treatment, we now had a vibe that potential donors could get excited about too. They could identify with the people we were; wives, parents, professionals and, everyday athletes no different than themselves. We had all come to competition relatively late in our lives; Ann had been competitive in college but hadn't done her first triathlon until age 36, Julie started at 41 and I returned to competition again at 48 with rowing and didn't race a bike until I was 56. Rainey also had a late start.

We began to look at ourselves as having an identity, a name and a look and it influenced our self-perception and translated into renewed effort. John was right, the momentum was building. Their contribution was a significant catalyst. Now we were rolling.

Chapter 6

A Mid-Stream Horse Change

Things were coming together. The training was going good – lots of green on my computer screen. We were branded and logoed. A website was up and functional. Donations began to trickle in. I had three good real estate listings and was working with several buyers. All the pieces seemed to be on track.

Rainey was the one who had engaged Jim Harper, who had taken videos of us riding and still shots to dress up the appearance of our website, which he also posted on YouTube and our Facebook page.

Eleven months from race start on July 21st, we had our first event. This was the wine tasting that Rainey had organized. It had been in the works when I was invited to join the team. This was a critical fund raiser in that the RAAM deadline for early registration was at the end of the month and the team's entry fee of $7,295 would be due then. Subsequent to that the fee would be ratcheted up by $1,100 for a month and another $900 after the first of the year and so on. Race organizers are fond of this penalizing pricing strategy for some reason.

Invitations had gone out to Rainey, Ann and Julie's contacts, but while I had decided to not invite anyone from my list, Mike, sent some out to a group of cyclists that we know, and to members of the rowing club we belong to, many of whom lived in the South Denver area where the wine tasting was being held.

Water2Wine was the establishment. This unique store is a winery that ferments its own wines from some 3 dozen grape varieties. Customers can select a single variety or blend from among them to be, crushed, fermented and eventually bottled with labels of their own design. For our party, guests paid an entry contribution and could taste several dozen different wines that the store offered. We collected a donation at the door, half of which went to the store. It seemed to work out quite well with 60 people showing up.

We had received a contribution of appetizers from Garbanzo's Mediterranean Grill, which Mike supplemented with some additional hor d'oeuvres that he picked up nearby.

But the real driver of the money we would take in that night would be from a variety of silent auction items that included two weeks at a 5 bedroom ski house in Vail, a variety of bike paraphernalia and apparel, restaurant gift certificates, chiropractic sessions, landscaping designs, apparel, a stained glass and so on. Among other things, I had signed up donations for training sessions at Peak to Peak Cycling, gift certificates from Turin Bikes, a massage at Solstice and a fung shui consultation from one of my co-workers.

We also sold a dozen or more Time Stations for $100 of which there were 55 along the RAAM race course. Buyers would receive a call from one of the support crew as we came through each station. These were identifiable locations about 60 miles apart, where teams were required to call in their time of arrival so that the organizers could track their progress and post team and solo rider positions on their website. People following the race could pull up the site and keep tabs on participants as they sped across the country.

Rainey had gotten a folk singer to provide background music and had recruited her chiropractor to be an announcer to introduce members of the team and make a pitch for the auction items and Time Station purchases. After introducing us all, he began an extemporaneous presentation that dwelled on the incredible difficulty of the race, which involves 170,000 feet of elevation gain.

"Thirty two miles straight up. That's like climbing Mt. Everest 6 times!" he blurted out with a pained expression on his face.

"We should probably try to talk them out of it. You have to be nuts to undertake the pain and suffering involved in this race", he continued, still wincing as if undergoing the torture himself.

I'm sure he meant that to come out in a commendable way, to emphasize the inspiration within the difficult nature of the race, but it sort of missed. I think in winging his comments, he got stuck in this suffering track and stayed there. But why would you ask someone to donate to a team that was taking part in a race they should be talked out of participating in?

Fortunately, I think everyone there glossed over his presentation, because in the end, the money raised that evening, added to what was already in the pot, was enough to cover the early entry fee. We were official. We were signed up. All we had to do now was to race it. Well, train for it and race it..... And pay for it.

And on that subject, Mike related an interesting conversation he had had that night with Rainey's husband, Michael Fritschen. There was a small room off to the side of the main wine tasting area that was used to display some of the auction items. Mike had put in a bid on a bike shop gift certificate and had come back to check and see if he was still high bidder.

Rainey's husband was an artist and had one of his lamp designs in the auction and was also there, checking to see what interest it was drawing. He looked up as Mike came in and offered a wan smile.

"Well this race is probably going to end up costing us a bunch of money out of our own pockets", he said looking down at the bid on his art piece and shaking his head.

Michael Fritschen's lament seemed to reflect that the elephant in his room was indeed large and taking up all the space.

We were making progress, but it was slow. And as we approached August, we concluded that it would be difficult to stage anything worthwhile until the fall. I was rowing in Oklahoma in August and then at FISA in early September and swamped with a large number of real estate transactions for one of JP Morgan's asset managers. The others were also busy. In September, Julie would participate in the Masters World Triathlon Finals in Beijing, while Ann and Rainey had kids home from school.

So I focused on throwing my own party in September, which would be followed by another Water2Wine event in November. John and Tasso were still coming up with clever promotional ideas and wanted to design an invitation for my affair. Tasso had used an old gothic styled script on our promotional T-shirts and practice jerseys. Stylistically, I thought it was interesting, but a little difficult to read. Nevertheless, invitations were printed up on dark orange paper using his gothic script. They were mailed out just after we left for Europe to several hundred people. It was scheduled for a week after we returned and was to feature a menu of beer and hotdogs. Mike was getting cases of a craft beer at cost and I was going to get a food truck offering gourmet hot dogs to park out front. We weren't going to charge for admission, in the hopes that donations would be adequate.

In hindsight, I probably should have concluded that the event was doomed. The timing made it difficult for us to monitor what response we were getting; the invitation sent a murky message which was difficult to interpret; and because I would be away, the

RSVP was to the Perry & Company receptionist. Further complicating things, the address was not for my house but one for an empty house that one of my associates had listed for sale 6 blocks away.

When we returned from Europe, we had no replies. And with only a few days left to try to scramble around and rescue the event, I decided to cancel it. I called and emailed everyone I could think of and asked my teammates to do so as well. But, Rainey was concerned that some of her friends might still show up. So, on the evening it was scheduled I went and sat in the empty house and waited in case someone did. One couple, who turned out to be friends of mine, did show up and while there was no beer and hotdogs, I came close to getting them to consider putting in an offer on the house.

So far, I had generated a rather thin resume in the fund raising department. First, I didn't invite my friends and acquaintances to the first wine tasting, because I was saving them for my own affair and then I had just canceled the damn thing, because no one on that list had replied. In addition, my contribution to the first silent auction was modest and, at that point, I hadn't received many hits on the LiveWell or LS&G donation web pages. So up to that point, I had been a total bust as a source of money.

This probably was a trigger point for Rainey. I had developed a nagging concern that she would end up dropping out. One of the reasons was that not long after I had joined the team, Rainey became very verbal in her criticism of me. I didn't quite understand what the issue was, but it was unsettling. Julie and Ann were baffled as well. Her being unhappy with me was not a good sign if we were going to be relay partners and share a bed during the race.

If her objective was trying to make me decide to quit as my predecessor had, she was dealing with the wrong person. I was all in up to my eyebrows; I was fully committed to doing RAAM. In the back of my mind, I thought when it was time to race, we would resolve this. Reasonable people can disagree, but they eventually find a way to work together.

But as the weeks wore on, and we came closer to the next Water2Wine evening, the dynamic between us didn't improve. On the positive side, our collection of silent auction items had been quite good and included a week's stay at a condo in Steamboat that Rainey herself had procured. The condo alone should have brought in several thousand dollars. Further, Rainey maintained that she was holding a total of $12,000 in contributions and combined with a similar amount the rest of us had put in the team checking account, we had a leg up on our way to hitting our $50,000 goal. My event had been rescheduled for the second week in December for which we were receiving positive responses and we had a number of other fund raising schemes in development.

But Rainey clutched. She pulled the plug. Everyone on the team received a call during which she tendered her resignation. Her reason wasn't the cost or a lack of training; it was the personality conflict between us.

This was a real blow. Initially, I was crushed. I felt badly that I was the cause of her decision. Throughout this whole period, I felt stunned that I was creating such apparent animosity. I really liked her as a coach. She was the one who had recruited me and I was touched by that. And here I was, being singled out as the bad guy. I took solace from the fact that I wasn't the first. Rainey was also abrasive toward the original fourth team member, Lark Birdsong, and her criticism caused Lark to quit. But now we needed to move on. We needed to look forward and focus on the positive. We needed to look for a replacement.

With Rainey's abdication, I thought I could find a candidate from among several strong riders who I knew. But Julie wanted to hold off as she went after the original fourth team member. Lark, in turn expressed interest, but couldn't commit and asked for three weeks to decide. Prior to her first RAAM in 2008, she had been active on the local master's bike racing scene, but since then hadn't competed. She had to convince herself to do another RAAM and to get back in training. My guess is Lark's initial reaction was negative. This is the kind of thing you have a visceral response to and get excited by the opportunity. Postponing a decision is not going to help, particularly after you've walked away from the same commitment 8 months previously.

In deference to Julie, for the next few weeks we remained in limbo, but in the end, Lark couldn't commit. So as we approached November, I began to mentally shuffle through my list. Athletic ability wasn't the only issue I was concerned with, financial ability was also. Rainey's contributions may not have been as firm as she let on and it may have been the underlying stumbling block for her. The team should seek to remove that risk in making the next choice.

My first target was, Lindsay Filsinger, a work colleague, who was an active cyclist and triathlete. It turned out I had previously planned a lunch date with her to see if I could get a contribution to the LS&G cause. She was expecting such a pitch, but instead I broached the idea of her joining the team. This caught her off guard, and she was floored. Her reaction was similar to mine when I was first asked. She was thrilled to be considered, just as I had been when first asked. But like me, she needed to think it over and discuss it with her husband. He, in turn, was positive as well and went so far as to meet with Joe Knopinski, to see what role he might play and if their personalities would mesh. I'm not so sure they did. In the end, with three young children still at home, the youngest being 3, they couldn't figure out the logistics and she withdrew from consideration.

While pondering which person to ask next, I gave Kathy Zawadski a call. I didn't want to go down a list of possible candidates and get a series of rejections. It wouldn't be good for someone to find out they were the tenth person asked. I had also broached the idea that Rainey wasn't going to make it to the starting line with her before. Kathy knew some of the same women I knew and she also had a number of training clients that might be viable candidates.

Her response was specific; she informed me she knew just the person.

"There's a woman in Salt Lake that I train," she said. "She's in her early 50's, in good condition; she competes some, and could easily deal with the cost of racing RAAM. I can send her an email and see if she's interested."

She then chided me about my meager adherence to her core and glute training sessions, but I regaled her with my rowing results in Poland and figured I was even. We said good bye and I hung up with the hope that this would lead to something, but also thinking, that we were looking at a short time frame for someone to get up to speed on this kind of commitment.

My concerns were unwarranted. Forty-five minutes later, there was a response. We were back to four.

Kathy forwarded me an email she had received, but not from her training client. It was from someone named Dina. Dina Hannah. Dina the Diesel.

It seems that Dina participated in the same high intensity spin class that the original email recipient did and was an endurance cyclist who had expressed an interest in RAAM. It got forwarded to her, she read it over a few times, had that same Eureka moment that all of us had in one form or another when first asked and decided to sign on – no questions asked! Dina's objective as an endurance racer was at some point to do RAAM solo. But in order to qualify as a solo rider, she would have to complete a qualifying event of which riding on a RAAM relay team was one. For her, it fit nicely into a longer term plan.

Dina at 48 was the right age to keep our average in the 50-59 age group. She was an executive at ARUP Laboratories as VP of Quality and Compliance which meant she probably had the financial capacity to do the event. Moreover, she was in good condition. She also had a great, feel good story about the benefits of cycling that would be ideal for LiveWell. It seems Dina had experienced a weight control problem and by the time she reached 40, weighed 240 pounds. It was then that she broke her foot. The doctor diagnosed the problem as a stress fracture caused by her excess weight.

She concluded that she needed to slim down. Her first approach was through a program of dieting, exercising and, after her foot healed, running. But after some initial success, an arthritic condition in her hip made running increasingly painful. As an alternative, she took up cycling. Her employer initiated a commuter challenge that encouraged bicycling to and from work, which she jumped at. Starting with a mountain bike she began to commute 15 miles to and from home. And those of us who enjoy cycling can find it to be addictive. She was no different and soon added miles in the evening and longer rides on the weekends and began to thoroughly enjoy the sport. She also began to lose weight as she had hoped. By the way, her new found activity earned the Salt Lake City Mayor's Gold Award for consistent bike commuting.

The distances got longer, she got thinner and faster, moved on to a road bike and joined a cycling club. She discovered she had an engine. And as it turned out, she developed a scratch she needed to itch. An award for commuting was fine, but to add validation of her new found sleekness, racing the bike was simply irresistible. So in 2008, four years after taking that first step to get fit, she entered the lottery to race the LOTOJA Classic and got selected. This is an annual 206 mile one day race from Logan Utah to Jackson Hole Wyoming that every year attracts a strong field of over 1,500 participants from all over the world.

Doing a race this distance would be a big step and she had concerns about finishing. To increase her worries, 3 weeks before the race, a drunk driver sideswiped her while she was riding. She bounced off the car but never crashed. She was able to remain upright on the bike despite the impact. However, she suffered a dislocated hip and bruising. A normal person at that point would throw in the towel; but not Dina. By race time the swelling was down, the hip in place and the pain minimal, so race she did. Some opportunities are just too hard to pass up. Dina, bad hip and all was rewarded by finishing 8th out of 26 finishers in the 25 - 44 year age group. She has done the race now 4 times and continues to see her times drop each year and in 2011 won the 45+ women's category at an average speed of over 20 mph!

She had now trained her sights on soloing RAAM. Dina had scant knowledge of who we were, but given the qualifying status of our entry, her response was easy. She was thrilled to have the opportunity to do RAAM and given her success as a racer, I was thrilled that she was going to be my partner.

As you might suspect everyone used Facebook to get their story out. Dina immediately added a second page for Dina Hannah RAAM Racer. And shortly her entries began to reflect a prodigious appetite for VOLUME! She provided entries throughout the weeks describing her indoor and outdoor efforts. Weekend rides of 100 miles or more were not infrequent. As we got closer to the start of RAAM she was entered in a lengthy endurance race that caused Julie to question her decision to take on risks of that nature. But, she was getting volume.

The second Water2Wine event was followed by a party I threw at the same house we had available for our failed effort in September. It was partially furnished making it ideal for a large event such as what we had planned and we had a terrific turnout that included many business colleagues, friends and past clients who lived in the area. We sold pretty much all the rest of the Time Stations, lots of commemorative t-shirts and took orders for the heart shaped chain ring pendants.

I was able to show progress in getting contributions from my friends and family. Mike had begun to contact some of his acquaintances and business associates and was seeing success as well. My 95 year old Aunt Louise chipped in generously as did my brother, Scott. I also lobbied them to bring a cheering section to the race course when we came through Illinois in June.

In February, an ice hockey buddy of Julie's husband, who owned the Blake Street Grill offered to share proceeds for a Super Bowl night with LS&G and in March, Marco's Coal Fired Pizza did a similar revenue sharing night. Slowly but surely, we chipped away at raising money. And up until the race started, we continued to receive donations allowing us to reach our race budget requirements and to contribute funds to LiveWell's programs. In the end Mike and I were responsible for bringing in one-third of the $55,000 raised. One elephant down.

Chapter 7

The Starting Line

This would be the 31st year in the event's history. It is promoted as the "World's Toughest Bicycle Race" and for the solo riders it certainly is. To be competitive, solo riders deal with very little sleep – last year's men's winner only slept 2 hours over the 8 days that he raced. They deal with muscle fatigue, saddle sores, hydration and calorie intake requirements that transcend what other endurance sports require.

The time record for solo men is 8 days 3 hours held by Bob Kish, who has finished the race 19 times. But the course varies in length from year to year, so Pete Penseyres who finished in 8 days 8 hours on a longer course holds the speed record at 15.4 mph. For a decade, it was principally thought of as an athletic endeavor for younger bodies, but, in 1990, the first man over 50 entered; in 1992, the first woman over 50 gave it a try and the following year an over 60 male competitor showed up. Since then competitors in their 50's through their 70's have been a constant feature, as the number of older entrants has grown each year with the number of relay teams.

Before the race in 2012, there have been over 2,700 entrants, but only 215 have been women. Of that, there have been only 8 women in their 60's. I would be the ninth and only four have been older than me. I was going to be in a pretty exclusive club if I made it.

The oldest at 69 has been Mary Brown of California, who was part of a mixed relay team 60-69 years of age. Patty Riddle at age 59 established an over 50 record with her partner in a 2 person mixed relay team but failed the following year to be the first woman to finish a solo attempt at age 60, so that's still on the table.

While solo racers are the endurance stars, relay racers have become a larger factor and now dominate entries. The first relay team was a 4 man in 1989 and in 2003, an 8 person relay team was allowed. Relay racers will do high heart rate interval bursts, while solo riders seek to conserve energy with a low heart rate over long periods of time. Relays are a less demanding side of the Race Across America, because by alternating riders and allowing for periods for recovery, the riders remain fresher and are able to produce higher speeds. The race record as one might imagine is held by an eight person relay team, Team ViaSat, an 8 man team, who would establish a new standard in 2012 by finishing the race in 5 Days, 5 hours and 5 minutes averaging 23.93 mph.

The record for women relay teams was set by Raw Milk Cats in 2011 of 19.22 mph or 6 days 11 hours and 34 minutes. This is the record for 4 women relay teams of any age and almost a full day faster than the previous mark for a 50-59 year old women's team. In order to eclipse that mark, LS&G would need to have some good luck, some favorable tail winds and plan for an efficient use of each rider's capabilities to maximize speed. Julie and Ann's Denver Spoke RAW team had been averaging close to 19 mph until they got into Colorado when they had to take longer pulls due to team weaknesses and ended with an 18:36 mph average. However, they set a finishing time record for that distance. With Dina and I as replacement riders, the conclusion was that, it was within the realm of possibility that LS&G could set a new time standard for RAAM.

It was on a Wednesday 3 days before the start when I reached Oceanside. Mike and Richie had driven the Audi Q5 from Denver and we were the first of the team to arrive. I had lounged in the back seat, in an effort to rest up as much as I could. I figured I was going to need it.

After checking into one of the motel rooms Mike had arranged for the team, we grabbed a late dinner. Mike chose an upscale restaurant near the beach for a celebratory last "good" meal in the belief that it would be a while before we would get anything other than racer fuel for the next week and a half.

After returning to our room and dropping into a sound sleep, the telephone rang. It was Joe asking Mike to come down and unlock the Audi. His brother Jack, who had been chosen to drive the RV had gotten it stuck turning into the motel driveway. The RV was mounted on a Peterbuilt truck body and unlike a bus style construction that has independently suspended wheels at the corners and a rear pusher engine, our "Super Nova" had a front engine and a drive shaft that connected to a fixed axle that placed the rear wheels about 18 feet from the back.

It provided sleeping arrangements for 10 people. There was a slide out portion that housed two bunk beds, a master bedroom, 2 banquets that slept 2 a piece and a space for 2 over the cab. Mike had located it at Hite RV Rentals near Denver and thought that given its large sleeping capacity it was the ideal choice. It would also enable the team to transport much of the crew and riders to the start and back from the finish and avoid the high drop off fees associated with a one way rental and the cost of flying the crew to the start and back from the finish. In fact, the group from Denver that came with it had room enough to stop near Salt Lake City to pick up Dina and Tyson Greenman, a bike mechanic with all his bike stand, tools and spare parts, on their way through.

But when they turned off the highway into the motel parking lot that night, the overhanging rear bottomed out on the crown in the middle of the highway, when the front wheels went up on the raised sidewalk crossing the entryway leaving the rear wheels in the gutter at the edge of the road. Thus with the weight on the front wheels and the tail end of the RV body, there was no weight on the rear wheels. Any effort to accelerate just spun the tires and generated smoke.

Jack had thrown some emergency equipment in the back of the Audi that included a hydraulic jack. This precipitated the phone call, which Mike answered and after fighting through the fog of sleep, he dressed and went downstairs with the car keys to retrieve it.

Unfortunately, the jack was small, not the industrial size you see at car repair shops. Given the monster size of the RV, it looked a little incongruous and ultimately proved woefully inadequate to resolve the problem. There then transpired a discussion regarding calling a tow truck, which would have to be one of those equally large units that probably cost an arm and a leg to get service from or to telephone the owner of the rental company for suggestions, although it was now about 3 am in the morning his time.

Finally, the conversation turned to lightening the rear end so as to put weight back on the tires. The freshwater storage tank which was full was located in the back and emptying it proved to be the salvation. Thus lightened, Jack backed the RV out on the highway with the guidance of his brother and several other of the crew who had broken out the crew's reflective vests and served as a cordon of ushers. It was decided that parking it along the curb was the preferred location and this was done. The team had met its first RAAM vehicle problem and had risen to the occasion.

By the time we got up for breakfast on Thursday it was warm and sunny with a fresh breeze. The typical California coastal morning overcast was not apparent by the time we gathered. We savored the pleasant weather knowing that when we left the coast, we were heading out toward climate regions much less sublime. Our conversation that morning was dominated by the plight of the RV stuck in the motel driveway, of how fast the Audi made it to Oceanside, and details on how the next several days would be spent.

Except for Dina's brother, John, who had been delayed, all the riders and crew were here. There was to be a total of 12 on the crew including Mike. The roles were pretty straight forward. There were to be 2 sets of driver/navigator teams for the two follow vehicles, a driver and navigator for the RV, a cook/masseuse and a mechanic; eleven people in all to support four riders. Joe and Bill Putnam would be 2 of the drivers, while David Lyons, Julie's husband and John Hannah, Dina's brother would be the other two. Their navigators would be Susan Griffin, who raced on the Denver Spoke's RAW team, the son of our next door neighbor, Richie Parkhill, along with 2 of Ann's friends, Paul Stranahan and Dave Ells. As mentioned, Joe's brother Jack was assigned the task of driving the RV, while Dina's friend Tyson, who ran a cycling race team support business in Salt Lake was his navigator and our mechanic. Rounding out the group was Michelle Wagner a friend of Ann's would be the cook and masseuse.

We planned to ride the first section of the course that day after which, we were to be interviewed by the RAAM organizers for a video spot that they would put on various social media touch points. We returned to the motel got dressed in our Santini kits and after discussing the route, grabbed our bikes and pushed off towards the course. The 2 follow vehicles, the Toyota van that Mike had rented from Hertz and the Audi set out to get their bearings as they were to take a separate route from the riders and to check out the first rider exchange point.

I took my back-up bike because I hadn't ridden it recently and wanted to make sure it was mechanically sound with the shifting dialed in. We picked up the race route several blocks from the motel where it follows the San Luis Rey River bike path. The path is used during the first part of the race to by-pass the busy parts of downtown Oceanside.

We were near the end of the path when we hit a steep little incline; I geared up to my biggest cog on my rear cassette and "clank", my chain locked up. Push as I might, my pedals wouldn't move. The chain had locked up on the gears. I came to a stop and got off, trying to work the pedals to move the chain. Nothing worked. It was jammed solid. The other girls continued on, while I called Richie in the Audi to come rescue me. They wanted to finish their reconnaissance, so there I sat for the next hour.

I was eventually rescued and when I returned to the motel, I brought the bike up to the room to Mike.

"The gears won't move, the chain seems to be jammed", I said.

He took it from me, turned it upside down resting it on the seat and handlebars and turned the crank. The chain clattered as it shifted onto a smaller chain ring in front and immediately started to spin the rear wheel.

"What did you do?" I asked dumbfounded by the seeming ease with which he got the chain unstuck.

"It's my fault", he said. "I put the same cassette on this wheel that is on your main bike. It has a 32 tooth large cog, but you have triple chain rings on this one and only a compact on your main bike, so not enough chain. Plus you're cross chaining."

This is a bad habit of mine. From time to time, I will shift to an easier rear cog and forget about shifting to a smaller chain ring in front, which a good cyclist should. This puts extra stress on the chain and on the gear teeth. This time when I did it the rear derailleur arm got fully extended and the chain got just got stuck. I hoped I wouldn't do this during the race. Mike was able to put a smaller cassette on and after traipsing to Alan's Bicycle shop to get some spacers so that it would work freely, I was set to go.

As for the RAAM video session, I missed it. We were one of the racer interviews conducted by the Race Director, George Thomas. It was being streamed in real time on their website and subsequently posted on the RAAM Facebook page and on YouTube. We had been accorded that honor because of the publicity and coverage the team had been able to generate, which the organizers were anxious to tap into. I had told a number of my friends about it and they were all disappointed when they tuned in only to be greeted with my empty chain and the 3 other LS&G riders. This was not an auspicious start.

Oceanside is now filled up with other teams with their vans and RVs all being outfitted with signage. Each vehicle had its Team number placard, ours was T411 / Love Sweat & Gears that was stuck on the front and sides of each vehicle, a yellow "Caution Bicycles Ahead" sign on the rear and various RAAM decals along with a set of yellow blinking lights for the vans roofs. Some vehicles, ours included, had extra decals of sponsors who had made monetary or in kind donations.

Motel parking lots were dotted with repair stands and bikes in various stages of being tuned or overhauled. Tyson was no different and was busy doing just that. In addition he added sealant to the tires. We added extra reflective tape to the frames and wheels, attached race numbers, I was T411B, and put on holders for bike lights. Once outfitted, bicycles and vehicles underwent inspections down in the parking lot near the start line by RAAM staff to see if they met up with specifications.

On Friday, we were one day from the start. Love, Sweat & Gears had become a media darling in Denver. The team and its RAAM quest had been featured multiple times in local TV sports casts and in articles written for several periodicals. Three of the local channels picked up coverage; Nick Griffith of Fox Sports, Doug Schepman of ABC and Suzie Wargin of NBC. We were also on an NBC program called Colorado & Company talking about our charity, LiveWell Colorado.

Competitor Magazine, a nationally distributed retail giveaway, did a page on us, as did several other local periodicals. But it was a Denver Post story on the front page of the OutWest living section devoting a half page to LS&G with a full color photo of us, that really had an impact. It was picked up by someone at NBC News, who thought it would be a good feature for the public interest segment usually done at the end of the Nightly News with Brian Williams broadcast. It got the green light and the producers committed a crew to follow us for the first several days and to meet us again at the finish.

This was great fun, our "15 minutes of fame". We met the producer Aarne Heikkila, reporter Michelle Franzen and their crew near race headquarters that morning for a film session. They had staged a set with chairs on the beach for interviews with all four of us that morning. The Pacific Ocean and the Oceanside Pier made up the background. Then, we went for a ride down a quiet side street while Michelle cycled with us and did a rolling interview with Julie. I think the uniqueness of our quest, our gender and our 50-something age made us great material. We couldn't have been more fortunate with the coverage we received and it certainly helped our fund raising efforts.

While we were doing this, the crew spent the day with Joe going through the official route book. They dutifully followed along and made notations in large notebooks created for each navigator. This exercise concentrated principally on the location of VMP's or vehicle meeting points of which there were to be 41. Some coincided with one of the 55 Time Stations, while others were picked because of their proximity to service stations. Joe had produced a colored satellite map page of each of the meeting points with details as to adjacent services - gas food, waste dumping stations, etc.

The emphasis on establishing fixed meeting points in advance was a concept that was adopted for the prior Race Across the West. It simplified the logistics of refueling and purchasing extra food, water and ice and had been established as a set strategy for this race. Joe had been diligent in his planning and had produced a color coded chart with vehicle and racer assignments for each segment of the race. It included distance and estimated times between meeting points that ranged from 46.1 miles and 2 hours 43 minutes on the low end to 100 miles and 5:59 hours on the high end for the first several days.

Mike sat in on these meetings. At the RAAM Crew Seminar he attended in December, there had been a recommendation by race officials of a race plan of 4 hours on and 4 hours off as a proven formula for a successful relay campaign. Joe and Bill made it clear that they didn't feel wedded to a strict 4 hour protocol.

Leading up to the race, Mike and I had expressed our opinions several times that we felt adherence to a 4 hour discipline was something the team should consider. However, there was never a serious response or an opportunity given for discussion. Now we were being presented with the specifics of their plan, which veered away from a 4 hour formula. Now, pre-determined vehicle meeting places were codified with glossy colored satellite maps with arrows and asterisks and circles and notations.

After the map work, the crew left for a RAAM presentation in the afternoon that included the introduction of various officials. This included someone who had previously competed as a racer and had been clipped from behind by a hit and run driver at 50 mph. When he didn't show up at the next rider exchange point, his crew backtracked to find him off the side of the road in the weeds in pretty bad shape. He spent the next 5 days in ICU. Also, while making the presentation George Thomas, excused himself to take a call, one of the solo riders, who had started on Wednesday had been in an accident. It turned out that despite being run over and dragged over by a vehicle, and requiring treatment at a hospital, he got back on the bike and continued. That was a sobering introduction to the risks the race entailed.

Later that afternoon, we all came back to the same auditorium for an Opening Ceremony during which all the teams were introduced. It was an emotional high. After all the obligatory introductions of past riders of note, they began to call up each team; two person relay teams including one from France, four person teams starting with the women which included us, and then the men with teams from Brazil, Germany, Australia, Slovakia, Great Britain, and finally 8 person teams.

Among the latter were the Wounded Warriors Project of the U.S. and Battle Back from the U.K. Both teams were comprised of wounded military veterans with a range of disabilities including paraplegics who rode hand cycles, some on recumbent cycles, others with prosthetic limbs who nevertheless rode standard bikes and some with brain injuries. You couldn't look at those men moving up to the front of the room without being moved by the sight. It was a humbling moment. I had seen a similar group of combat wounded veterans before. Mike had ridden with a USO sponsored Ride2Recovery group of over 30 riders when they came through Colorado several years ago and I watch them start out on their ride one morning. It was truly an emotional experience.

Chapter 8

Race Day

Oceanside, CA Race Time 0:00 Miles 0.0

It's now Saturday morning, Race Day. Mike and I woke a little before 7:00 am and began the process of packing up. I had slept fitfully. An elephant showed up. Old Fear of Failure anxiety had gotten a little bigger in the middle of the night. On top of which, I had an upset stomach. I couldn't tell if it was from all my anxieties or the prior night's restaurant selection.

But once I was fully awake, the worries began to recede as I folded and stuffed gear and apparel into my bags. The immensity of the adventure ahead now took top billing, which summoned a new emotion: impatience. I had an intense desire to get on with the race. I'd done the training, the bike was tuned, the tires pumped, the gear bags packed and everything was ready. All I wanted to do was get on the bike and ride. But I had to wait and fidget. There was still over 6 hours to survive before I could clip in and push off.

By 8:00 we had finished getting reasonably organized, left the bags in the room and went downstairs. Members of our crew were in a small guest sitting area near the front desk, the Race organizers had made a number of last minute route changes that needed to be added to the navigation instructions. Summer is road construction time and the need for race route detours was not uncommon. Joe had copied the handwritten changes and was handing them out.

There was a box of sticky buns, some orange juice and coffee for the crew, while the four racers planned to go off by ourselves for breakfast. Julie and Ann were already there in the room and Dina soon followed.

We left the crew to their route changes at the motel and started walking up the street to get breakfast at Carrow's Restaurant. Tyson was in the parking lot working on a bike that was up on a stand with his tools spread all around him. He had finished injecting liquid sealant into the inner tubes and was now madly spinning a bicycle crank and clicking through the gears to make sure the bike was still tuned.

Several other teams were staying at the motel and their crew members were loading gear in a half dozen support vehicles festooned with sponsor logos, team signage, RAAM stickers and caution warnings.

The day was already clear and sunny as the usual overcast or "marine layer" that normally hangs around until early afternoon wasn't there. Being greeted by such wonderful weather would seem to be a good omen of things to come.

But clear skies in the morning on a California beach in June can often mean that Santa Ana atmospheric conditions were prevailing. So instead of the normal offshore breezes from the west keeping cooler moist ocean air over coastal regions and creating overcast; there were dry winds coming from a high pressure system over the desert pumping hot air over the mountains from the east pushing the moisture away. These conditions create the winds that fan California's wild fires and they could create head winds for us when we started our journey if they remained. For now at least, the winds were light.

We all slid into a booth and began to look over the menu. The waitress came, and when it was my turn, I ordered a bowl of oatmeal and fruit with some yogurt and green tea. This, I thought would help my stomach, while giving me enough fuel for the upcoming ride.

There should have been a sense of excitement, some giddiness or a charged energy as we were about to embark on the race, but instead the mood was tense and edgy. Topics of conversation involved how much sleep one got, whether all the packing was done and similar banalities.   Race-wise the major topic was laundering our riding apparel regularly so that we would have fresh shorts to wear and hopefully avoid saddle sores.

While Julie and Ann had ridden the first part of the race during RAW, we didn't talk about the demands of the route; how long were the climbs, which were the toughest or how hot did it get? We were all impatient and wanted the race to start. This may have contributed to a reticence to dwell on such details.

After breakfast, we went back to our rooms to change into riding apparel and finish packing. While the crew was only allowed one bag each, racers had 6 changes of cycling apparel, the four Santini outfits, club and LS&G training jerseys and shorts plus jackets, vests, leg and arm warmers, extra shoes, an extra helmet, rain gear and so on. We would be a rolling Lycra show room.

When Dina and I got to the RV to stow our gear, most all of the storage space in the only bedroom was already in use. The RV had initially been parked at Julie's house and she and Ann had first dibs on the closets. The room wasn't that big and the bed took up much of the area, but with some ingenuity, we were able to cram our gear under the bed, in various cubbies and corners, in the slide out bunk area and as a last resort, shoved on the floor.

For the next week, this would be our home.

By 10:30 we had finished with the RV and I now went to my follow vehicle, the Audi, with a large plastic milk crate filled with my helmet, shoes, extra clothes, clear glasses, primary and spare bicycle lights and charging cords, a big plastic jar of energy drink powder, Honey Stinger waffles and Mix One protein shakes, and a roller I use for tight muscles. I also had a cooler I would fill with a bag of ice, perishable food and extra water and importantly what would become my go to, primary staple, a peanut butter and jelly sandwich.

Dina and I were to be the first pair of riders on the road. I was not going to take part in the starting ceremony, but rather, Paul, Richie and I were going to drive to the first rider exchange point beforehand. Most of the other teams participated in the start together and rode a short distance on the controlled speed part of the race course. It was a memorable part of the event and would be the last real bonding experience racers would have until Annapolis. Except for brief moments at team exchanges, relay racers wouldn't see half their teammates for the rest of the race. But, it was determined that Dina would ride it alone.

Our start time was 12:11 PST; we would be the 11th team out the gate. The distance to the first allowable rider exchange point was not quite 24 miles. There were pace riders for the first third of that so Dina probably wouldn't arrive until 1:40 pm or so. While we would have had plenty of time to watch the start and make it to the exchange point in time, the rationale was not to risk getting stuck in traffic or succumb to some other issue. So at 11:30, I got in the van with my crew to drive to the first exchange point and wait.

Mike was asked to make sandwiches for the initial two driver-navigator support crews. He determined that this would have kept him bottled up in the RVs kitchen before the start of the race, which he wanted to observe, so he opted to dart across the street and buy four turkey sandwiches from a coffee shop, which he put in each of the follow vehicle coolers along with fruit, snacks and cookies.

It proved not to be the best choice because as we moved across the country, the frequency of turkey sandwiches on the menu and the amount of mayonnaise thereon became a contentious subject. This was in contrast to the Fuzzy Mitchell simplicity dictum that resulted in turkey sandwiches being the only item on the menu. He believed it to be the most efficient solution for purchasing food inventory, for meal preparation and for healthy nutrition. But such was not to be our fate.

When he had finished the lunches, he walked down to the start area. Instead of going in the RV to the first team exchange in Borrego Springs, he had cadged a ride with Jim Harper, who would follow the race in a rental van in which he had installed shelves and bins to hold his photography equipment. He could also jury rig the sliding door to get pictures alongside the racers while underway. John Marchetti, who had been terrific at generating media coverage for the team, had volunteered to be his driver. Jim had an intense and exacting personality, while John was more laconic and somewhat slow and deliberate in his actions. They were a contrast in personalities.

The scene at the start area was kaleidoscopic. That the day was so delightfully sunny had to have been a factor. People under the Oceanside Pier collected in small groups of team and crew in their multicolored kits. Others, including Mike's sister, lined the bridge leading out to the pier that passed over the Strand just before the start line.

There was a hum of nervous conversation, occasional laughter, shouts and impromptu photo sessions. Mike moved from group to group, talking with racers, giving a thumb's up and wishing good speed. At one point he was buttonholed by a huge 6'6" German, who when he heard Mike was from Denver had to recount a lengthy story about his travels Colorado and in particular, the Rocky Mountain National Park and the people he met there.

The anticipation building up had everyone bubbling with energy. And until the racers got on the road there was a release of it through verbal and social interactions. Giddiness, excitement and nervousness were all on view. No one seemed to be showing any apprehension over what lay ahead; 100+ degree temperatures, rain, accidents, injuries, mechanicals, fatigue and whatever else 3,000 miles of secondary roads in rural America can throw in the way.

Suddenly, a half hour before noon, a P.A. system hummed and squawked and then amplified George's voice. The crowd quieted down and began to press in. He started with a series of introductions, which included several event winners and record holders from the early years, and a short interview with the celebrity basketball player and sports commentator, Bill Walton. Mike said Bill has gargantuan feet and wore a pair of enormous basketball sneakers, which seemed incongruous when compared with all the sleek shiny bike shoes of the racers.

Finally, the clock moved to 11:55. The first honorary pace riders rolled up to the start and got their introductions, then George called Team T200 to the starting line. It's Dream Team 115, a two man - under 50 relay team from Germany. They both roll up to the start. George asks them their names, gives them some encouraging bromides and then starts a count down.

"Four, Three, Two, One, Go....

Its 12:00 noon, and they're off.

There is a cheer from the crowd as they head north along the Strand for four blocks until turning east with their backs to the Pacific Ocean. We would pass them 270 miles into the race before Time Station Number 4 in Parker, Arizona.

Next up were the Flying Hosers, Team T201. This was an under 50 mixed team that was very good and very fast. We would trail them all the way across the country until the Appalachians and caught them outside of Rouzerville, PA, with only 140 miles to go and would beat them by 3 hours.

Several more two man teams rolled up and started off. Then it was time for the 4 person teams. First up was Team T402, Equipe Hupert Schwarz. This was a 50-59 age team of German men whom we would chase all the way across the country. At one point before Pagosa Springs, Colorado with Dina and me on the road, we would pass them, only to get passed back before reaching Alamosa. They would beat us to the finish line by less than 2 hours.

As each minute went by, a new team would roll up to the start line. George would get them to say a few words. Most go off four abreast including T410, the Hunky Dory Renegades from Ireland, who left the start line just before us.

Then Team T411, Love Sweat & Gears, came to the line. Dina is the only one on her bike. Ann and Julie are jogging beside her.

"All right", he announced, "Boy, we now have the media darling team. We're happy to have you here. You're going for the 50 plus record, right?"

George pushed the microphone at Julie.

"Absolutely", she responded.

Then after getting similar assurances from Dina and Ann, he said, "With that excitement, I'm sure you're going to make it. Okay, you're taking off in ten seconds."

He turned away to clear a path and continued, "....It all comes down to this, now. The clock starts in five, four, three, two, one....."

And at 12:11 PDT, Dina pushed down on her pedal, swung her other foot up to clip in, rose up out of her saddle to accelerate and headed down the Strand between 2 rows of applauding spectators.

"Go Dina! Woo hooo!" a voice in the crowd called out amidst the cheers.

The Toyota van, which would be Dina's support vehicle, fell in behind. She turned right on Surfrider Way and headed uphill for several blocks then left. Here the Toyota continued straight and wouldn't pick her up until she had completed the first 23.8 miles. After a half mile she turned onto the Bike Path, on which there would be no passing allowed until the end at mile 7.8.

The path took her east on an old railroad right of way along the wide flat bottom of the San Luis River a source of water the local Luiseño Indians called Quechla. She would pass to the north of the old Mission of San Luis Rey de Francia, which was founded in the late 1700's. It was one of the largest of the early California missions covering nearly 1 million acres.

It was also the western terminus of a major Indian trail that connected with the inland valleys of the Coastal Range and to the Imperial Valley beyond. When the Spanish first arrived the area had a population of 5,000 Luiseños Indians, but European diseases and harsh conditions at the missions dropped this number in half by the early 1800s and by 1910 only 500 survived.

Dina would have no crew support in case of a flat or mechanical problem, although such a risk was slim. She also had to memorize the half dozen turns as there would be no navigation support behind her. Dina did end up missing one turn, but was fortunate to recognize her error quickly and was able to turn around and get back on course.

After leaving the path, there is no speed restriction just a 600 foot climb up Morro Hill from mile 10 to mile 13 along Sleeping Indian Road. This is California living at its best. Dina would pass tasteful mission style homes, decorated with bougainvillea shrubs, stands of date and fan palms amid groves of avocado and citrus. The seductive warm California sunny beach day that we started out with was still there. It was like a soft good-bye kiss from a loved one before going off to war. It wouldn't be long before weather conditions like as this would be a wistful memory.

I was up ahead at our first rider exchange point near Valley Center on the road to Mount Palomar. There was a large collection of RAAM support vehicles at the Castle Road parking lot, the point at which teams could make their first rider exchange. Most will switch riders here and Paul decided we should go up the road a ways to give ourselves room.

For the most part Paul, Richie and I sat in the car and exchanged small talk occasionally looking at the clock. When we left Oceanside to drive inland, I could feel the temperature begin to rise. And now, as we sat there waiting for Dina, it continue to get warmer.

At one point, I got out of the car and walked up the road, away from the vehicles and into a wooded area. I found a bushy juniper to hide behind for my inaugural RAAM al fresco pee. What a pain. I peed on my right shoe.

In schooling myself for the race, I watched a DVD that followed RAAM in 2005. For the first 2 days of that race, the lone woman solo rider, Cat Berge had stayed up with a half dozen of the fastest male soloists, but then began to fall back. Part of her explanation was that men were able to relieve themselves much faster with a need for less privacy than women. I would have ample opportunity to experience the reason for Cat's observation and hopefully in the future, avoid my shoes.

Finally, at a little after 1:00 pm, Jim Harper's van pulled into the Castle Road parking area. Mike got out and came up the road looking for me. When he reached the Audi he poked his head in, gave me a big smile.

"This is it", he said. "No turning back now. It's ON!"

"Finally! What a relief to finally get this thing underway," I said.

With Mike showing up, it meant that Dina couldn't be far off. I climbed out of the car and took my bike from Richie who had taken it off the rear bike rack. I peered back down the road in the direction Dina would come from to make sure I wouldn't miss her. Follow vehicles from all the other teams were clustered in the nearby parking lot and strung out on the road. We had already seen the faster riders come past with new riders starting out at the first exchange point. It was the beginning of a parade of spandex gypsies and their crews that would relentlessly move eastward over the next week in search of Annapolis.

Mike had his iPhone out taking a video and was asking me questions so he could post a clip on the team website and on Facebook. I tried to respond, but my adrenalin was pumping. I was anxious for Dina to show and on being ready for the exchange. My answers showed that distraction as I kept looking back down the road for Dina. Another RAAM rider passed our location.

I peered toward my crew in the Audi. They were talking on the radio with the other follow vehicle.

"Is she coming?" I asked.

Finally, Paul's head popped out.

"Joe radioed that she made the turn on Castle Road", he said.

It won't be long now. We were about a half mile from that turn. There was a bend in the road about 200 meters from where we were waiting, shaded by a big live oak. Finally, through the tree, I could see the light blue team jersey appear. Dina's head was bobbing as she worked the pedals up the moderate grade. When she was 50 meters away, I turned to look at the road that lay ahead, took a deep breath, pushed down on my pedal and began to gather speed.

"Go, Amy, go!..... Go now!" I heard behind.

I pushed to up my tempo. Dina overtook me after 20 meters and I dug in hard. Finally, I was in the race. I built my speed up, dropped onto my aero bars and got into a rhythm. I had all this energy stored up and felt that I could hit it pretty hard, but at the same time all I could think was the enormity of the distance in front of me. There seemed to be a need to save some of my energy. I envisioned a huge map of the United States and I was this little dot way on the left-hand side with Annapolis way on the right side of the continent. It seemed immense. But then I thought to tell myself, one pedal stroke at a time. And so I began my journey across the country in the tracks of those who preceded me.

In the meantime, Dina had gotten in her follow vehicle and gone up the road for her next pull. Richie and Paul were somewhere behind me. Support vehicles were not allowed to follow directly behind the rider, due to State Police stipulations. This required the driver to come up behind his rider, pull over and wait for a minute or so and then repeat in a leap frog fashion.

During the first 29 years of RAAM, a support vehicle with flashing lights followed right behind each rider. But beginning last year, California, Arizona and Colorado, the first 3 states the race passes through, outlawed this practice during daylight hours over the concern that normal road traffic could get stuck behind and lead to unsafe attempts to pass on the secondary roads the race follows.

So the normal strategy is to pull to the side of the road, which allows for normal traffic to pass, before catching back up. Alternatively, one could pull ahead of the rider as well and wait for her or him to go by. If something happens to the rider, such as happened to the hit and run victim introduced at the Crew Seminar, it could be some time before the crew would recognize a problem and retrace their steps.

This had happened to us once when we were training for the race. During a rider transition practice, Joe had passed me and turned off the course at the top of a hill with the objective of doing a quick U-turn to get behind me when I passed. The problem was, I was faster than they expected, and by the time they had executed their turn around, I had already passed their location. So there they sat, looking back down the hill.

"Where's Amy?"

At least it pointed out the flaw of getting ahead of the rider and led to the team's adoption of a "stay behind" rule for the first 3 states.

The road was narrow with a minimal shoulder. There were trees shading the road. We passed large homes with immaculate white fences around pastures. Above us were foothills with bushy sagebrush and avocado and citrus orchards higher up. Outcroppings of white granitic rocks interspersed with brush cluttered near the top. The temperature was now in the high-80's, not too hot yet.

As I rode, the upset stomach, the anxiousness and the waiting were now behind me. Hundreds of hours and thousands of miles of training in the last year were now being put to task. Getting on the bike and turning the pedals was a joy. I was elated. I tried to take in what I was passing through, to absorb it; the views, the physical sensations of riding, everything.

After several miles, the road tipped up at 6% and I began a climb of 700 feet. This would continue for another 2 miles and Dina would take over at the top where it flattened. As I began to feel the grade in my legs, I got out of the saddle to maintain my tempo.

I was feeling good from the effort. My conditioning was there, the grade was manageable. It was liberating. I came under a stand of eucalyptus and looked up the road where it began to flatten and could see cars parked on the side ahead. Other teams were changing riders here.

Just then the Audi pulled around and passed me and up ahead, I saw the Toyota minivan and Dina, standing in front looking back. She turned and started riding when I got near; I passed her on the inside and began to slow down as she bent to the task.

"All right, Amy!" I heard Mike yell. He had been standing up the road from where I stopped taking a few photos. He clenched his fist and shook it.

"All right!"

The Audi had stopped behind the Toyota and Paul had come up to pick up my bike and put it on the rack. I headed to the car for a drink. We didn't carry water bottles on the bike. No need for the extra weight, but we did carry a small under seat bag with a spare tube and CO_2 inflator. Mike always questioned the necessity of this with a crew behind me to fix flats, he thought I should strip all unwanted weight off the bike, but I followed everyone else's lead.

I relaxed in the back seat and drank ice water from a Camelback water bottle and reflexively nibbled some trail mix. I harbored a concern that I would not consume enough calories and that led me to take a handful of food even though I had only gone 4 miles. It was a great reinforcement to know that regardless of how tough and demanding the cycling became, after each effort on the bike, I could take refuge and eat, drink and recover in the car. As I would soon learn, it would at times be just enough to keep me in the game.

On my second pull, I caught a sharp descent that flattens out near a sprawling Harrah's Casino Resort. We're in Indian country now, on the Rincon Reservation. As a legacy to the development of the California missions, there are many Indian reservations scattered throughout the southern part of the state; sixteen in San Diego County alone. We will pass near 5 of them before we descend to the desert. Many were established in mid and late 1800's after California became a state, but the right to irrigate with water from the Quechla wasn't granted until 2010.

We were riding 5 miles between exchanges and except for shortening up on steep climbing areas and increasing it for descents; that proved to be the formula we would follow for the rest of the race. From Castle Road, it was another 33 miles to the first Time Station at Lake Henshaw with 3,500 feet of climbing and 1,000 feet of downhill. The time recorded by Raw Milk Cats the prior year was 3:28. Dina and I came through at 3:39, 11 minutes off.

After Henshaw, the route turns north east toward Warner Springs on the east side of the lake. The Santa Ana winds were there waiting for us. We had been riding in a southwesterly direction and it had been a side wind before, but now we were getting it right in the face. I was on the bike then, and I had to gear down into an easier ratio to maintain a good cadence.

To the north of us was the town of Temecula, with gently rolling hills and numerous springs. It lies far enough inland to be beyond the coastal overcast and takes its name from the Luiseños village of Temecunga, or "where the sun breaks through the mist".

Temecula lies on a natural travel route and was the site of the first Post Office south of San Francisco established when the Butterfield Overland Mail started operations in 1857. When we turned east out of the headwind on the San Felipe Road we would be riding the old Butterfield stage road. It connected St. Louis to San Francisco on a circuitous "oxbow" route that went through Texas, crossed the Colorado River at Yuma, and continued through Mexico before turning north toward where we were now.

John Butterfield went bankrupt after a few years and his stage line and mail contract was taken over and reorganized by Wells Fargo. The subsequent bank's iconic brand and foreclosure activities remain to this day.

We turned off on Montezuma Valley Road and the grade began to increase, rising another 1,400 feet before hitting the top of the San Jacinto Mountains past the little town of Ranchita. Farther on, the horizon began to flatten and before long, the road began to descend. Then, rounding a corner, the near horizon dropped away and one could see the desert stretching far into the distance some 3,000 feet beneath us. Below to the left was the town of Borrego Springs and in the distance the Santa Rosa Mountains the color of dusty beige and beyond the Salton Sea. It was a breath taking view.

I had taken us to the heights past Ranchita and Dina took over from there descending the 9 mile "Glass Staircase" down to

Borrego Springs where there would be the first team transition. While dramatic, racers weren't there for the view and with an 8% grade they were staring wide eyed at the road with rapt attention as speeds reached above 50 mph in some sections. Dina's Garmin showed that she had hit 48 mph. The daredevils were overtaking the cautious while leapfrogging support vehicles added to the drama. And as the careening riders descended, the temperature climbed toward 100°.

John followed Dina in the photo van. He was pulling over and allowing cyclists and support vehicles to pass him, being extremely cautious as was his nature. Dina pulled farther ahead, but John remained circumspect and gingerly followed behind. Mike, however, was anxious to get to the team exchange and be there to towel me off. It was tough, but he held his tongue and accepted John's driving style in silence. Jim was quiet too, but also seemed impatient.

When we reached the RV a mile or so passed Borrego, we had left the high chaparral of the San Jacinto's at 4,220 feet and were on the desert floor at 800 feet. Borrego is the Spanish word for the big horn sheep that are found in the area. It was given the name by Juan Batista De Anza when he established the overland route from Mexico through the Sonoran Desert in the 1770's. The first expeditions to settle Alta California came by sea and took several perilous months, because of prevailing winds and the southern flow of the California Current, otherwise it required a 3 month march through the difficult terrain of the peninsular mountains and deserts of Baja with limited water and pasture.

In the first attempt to colonize San Diego, over half the Spanish exploration team that started out died from scurvy or thirst before getting there. Some of those that made it were subsequently killed in Indian raids. Clearly, in those early years, it wasn't the alluring tourist destination that it is today.

The De Anza route went through northern Mexico toward present day Tucson following the water courses of the Santa Cruz River north and then the Gila River west to the Colorado. But from there they needed to cross desert in a northwest direction toward the Coastal Range.

On his first expedition, after trying a route lacking water and forage that led into sand dunes, De Anza backtracked and turned towards Borrego and after several days found water in nearby Coyote Canyon. On his second trip in 1775, leading a company of thirsty settlers and livestock across the desert toward the Canyon water source, a heavily pregnant woman in this party noticed a white quartzite outline of a human figure on a mountain that appeared to be a pointing in its direction. She declared it to be a miracle, an angel pointing to water.

The following day was Christmas Eve and the woman, Gertrudis Rivas, gave birth, beside the gurgling stream, to the first white European child born in California.

After resting Christmas Day and replenishing with water she got on her feet and continued on with the rest of the company over the San Jacinto Mountains and down the other side to the San Gabriel Mission. Five years later, traveling the same trail, the first 11 families would come to establish the pueblo of Los Angeles. And over this route, 238 years later, we rode southeast into the Sonoran Desert from whence they came.

Borrego Springs - 85.8 miles - 5:10 hours

Chapter 9

Sonoran Desert

Dina had done the first 23 miles of the race solo, and we had shared the remaining 63 miles. She was aggressive on the descents like the "Glass Staircase" and would take a large share of them. We wouldn't do an exchange until one of us reached the bottom so as not to waste momentum. So throughout the race, I seemed to get a full share of climbing and less of the descents, although, given my seniority, that seems counter-intuitive. So when I reached the RV, I had built up a good appetite.

After changing into a t-shirt and skirt, I returned to the kitchen area for a meal of Spanish rice and chicken breast from the large store of meals that had been pre-prepared and frozen before the trip.

It was here that Mike and I started a ritual. He would pull my bike off the rack on the Audi if Dina was finishing up a segment or directly from me if I was the finisher. Quickly look it over before putting it on the rack on the rear of the RV and then join me inside. He would then ask me how the ride went, if there were any problems with the bike, and make sure I ate.

My history with him was that he was the guy who said "yes you can" when I asked, "can I do it?" This was a question and response ritual that had started after we met in Denver in 1994. I had been living in Albuquerque, New Mexico, back then, when I received a call from an old East Coast friend inviting me to drive up to Denver and join him to play golf. I had finished a course in Fine Arts at the University of New Mexico, had put my house on the market and was planning to move back to the St. Louis area to help out my mother in the family oil business before deciding whether to return to New York, my previous residence, or to San Francisco where I had lived in the 80's.

But before golf, much to my initial annoyance, my friend had to have lunch with one his business acquaintances. It was Mike. As we talked that day, it turned out that we had a number of mutual friends that we both knew from our years working in New York. I recalled that I had heard his name mentioned before as someone who had dropped out of Wall Street and moved to Vermont to ski, which I thought was kind of gutsy.

He struck me as being calm and comfortable with himself. His stories took forever, but he sounded smart and had a nice way of speaking. What also intrigued me was that over the following weekend, he was going to compete in a race involving rowing a single shell across Lake Dillon, which is at 9,000 feet in elevation, jump on a bike and circle the lake and then row back to the start. This was not the ordinary weekend pursuit for someone in his 50's

The whirlwind affair that began when he tracked me down 3 months later ended in marriage 2 months after that. While that is the subject of another story, what entered my life was a relationship with someone who enjoyed an active lifestyle that included competitive sports and who encouraged the same thing for me. Needless to say, I was game. And while a physically active person, I hadn't competed athletically in years. After meeting Mike, things began to change. It started with skiing. He coaxed me away from my comfort zone on green and big wide blue ski runs, onto black diamonds.

As he urged me onto ever more difficult trails, I would ask, "Can I do it?"

The answer always came back "Yes". Always.

Mind you, there were times teetering on a mogul in some chute he dragged me into, that I would question his wisdom. Staring at the drop in which I needed to make a turn, it could take a minute or so to work up the courage to do it, but I would. I would make the turn. And I would go back again.

Six months into our marriage, he announced he was going off to Minnesota for a week to race in the U.S. Rowing Masters Championships. This made me envious. He brought home a gold and a silver medal, which made me even more jealous. I reached a conclusion that I could sit on the beach and watch or I could learn to row myself.

The following spring, he began to teach me to row. He started out by putting me in the bow seat of a double scull and said, "Do what I do". After several months of trying to follow his movements (and having a few heated conversations), I ventured out in a single scull; first in stable recreational boats and then in a racing single. He had planned to row in the Canadian Masters Nationals Regatta on Elk Lake on Vancouver Island in August and suggested that I was ready to do a race too.

He planned to enter me in 3 sprint races 1,000 meters in length; a novice single, a recreational single and a mixed double with him. By that time I had only rowed a single 8 times previously and when he told me the plan, I was apprehensive. Anyone who has rowed in a racing single knows how sensitive the boats are and that they require good rowing technique to provide stability. Here I was rowing in a National Championship event that draws competitors from all over Canada and the U.S., I knew I could do it, but I didn't want to embarrass myself and look foolish.

So I asked again, just to make sure, "Can I do this?"

As expected his answer was, yes, and so I entered.

Our first event was the mixed double. It was a good race to start with because with a two person crew there are four oars on the water providing better stability. And I had rowed with Mike many more times in a double than I had in a single. So off we went.

The start of the race was in the middle of the lake and the finish near shore because of the prevailing west to east wind. We rowed way out into the middle and did a couple of practice starts, which are always a little tricky as you work to get the boat up to speed quickly. Then they called our heat and we rowed into our lane and backed up to a small platform on which a teen age girl lay on her stomach. She grabbed the stern of our boat and we waited for all the boats to get aligned. Finally, an amplified voice polled the crews calling out each of their club names.

Then it said, "Attention..........Row!

There were six boats in our race and we all started furiously pushing our legs down and pulling in on the oars. The race was on. After the first couple of quick strokes we began to take longer ones to accelerate the boat. Four strokes, five, six, seven......and then my right oar slipped away. Something was wrong. It was flopping around and I couldn't pull it out of the water. Mike's oar clashed against it. He looked over at the oar then back at me. We glided to a stop.

The button on my port oar, the round part that keeps it snug against the oarlock had popped off. There was no way that one could row effectively without a secure button; certainly not me. Nevertheless, I felt awful. I felt terrible. I had ruined our chance.

Of course, it wasn't my fault. Buttons can be moved to change the oar's leverage, but once moved are always tightened back down with a bolt. Someone missed this last step. Not my fault, but my lack of experience made me think I was to blame.

So with this opening act, I entered the novice single. The button on my oar held this time and I found myself in second place coming down the course until the last 200 meters when those west winds moving closer to shore made for choppy water. It was then that I experience a heart gripping error – a boat stopping "crab ". This occurred at the finish of a stroke as the boat slewed in the chop, causing one oar to go too deep and get stuck in the water. As I tried to pull the oar up, the boat instead tipped precipitously on edge. Fortunately, I recovered and managed to get the boat moving again, but had fallen back and only managed fourth place.

How could I face Mike? I was so embarrassed to have rowed so poorly. Not once but twice! Yet there he was there at the dock telling me how proud of me he was and what a great recovery I had managed, which helped some, but I was still crestfallen.

After putting the boat away, the public address announcer said that medals for the Novice Single were about to be given. "And in third place, all the way from Denver, Colorado, is Amy Shonstrom!"

Having only been married a short time, I was unused to that name, so initially, I thought, "Gee, that name sounds familiar. "

Then it dawned on me that they were calling me up to the podium. This created a whole new perception to the event. It was an age handicapped race and my competitors were mostly younger women. So in an instant, I went from defeated to medal winner. It was the first award I'd received since being a kid at summer camp. I was beaming.

That first race took place in 1996 and since then, I have rowed in many regattas all around the world with excellent results. This has included gold medals from annual trips to the US Masters Nationals and from FISA International World Masters events in Europe and Australia. During this time, I immersed myself in the sport, and served as president of my local rowing club, founded a separate national club for elite women and served on the US Rowing Masters Board of Directors.

My introduction to bicycle racing was less dramatic than was that first regatta. Mike and I had always included cycling as a cross training exercise for rowing. We started with mountain bikes, but switched to road bikes after Mike went over the handlebars and separated a shoulder on a particularly nasty descent. We had done a lot of Colorado's classic climbs and participated in a few centuries, but the real catalyst was a bike tour we signed up for in Europe 8 years ago.

We were entered to row in the FISA Masters in Vichy, France and Mike found a tour that started the following week tracking stages of the Vuelta de Espana through the Pyrenees. Except for me and two of the guides, the group consisted of men. Most of them were bike racers. Their ranks included Frankie Andreiu, who had ridden with Armstrong on the US Postal team and David Haase, who had soloed RAAM. You would think that getting dropped so quickly, so often by the rest of the group would have been a negative, but it was an eye-opening trip.

Our tour group rode the race route before the start, which was lined with spectators. Often, I was saluted with shouts of "Viva la femme!" or "bon courage!" as I rode by and occasionally, on steeper pitches, a helpful fan would run out and push me along. On most days, we would stop at the top of one of the mountain passes for lunch and watch the racers as they went over. If you've got any competitive juices at all, the festivities and excitement of a grand tour are going to have a big influence on you. It did me.

The next year, Mike turned 65 and seeing as there were a series of races for that age, he decided to join a bike club and give it a try. His first effort would be the relatively short, 4.5 mile, Lookout Mountain Pillar to Post Hill Climb, that took place on a road on which we often trained. As the time grew closer to the event, my desire to race it also grew and once again, I asked him "can do it".

When the day of the race came, it was drizzling rain and raw, the kind of weather that would normally keep a sane person indoors. But, I was so anxious to try a race, to see how well I could do, that

I was oblivious to the conditions. And just as in my first rowing race, I took the third place prize in the citizen's class. Not a medal this time, but a home-made chocolate layer cake. That, as they say, was the frosting.

So at age 56, I began racing my bike competitively. Along the way, I've ridden Team Evergreen's iconic 120 mile, Triple By-Pass Ride in Colorado, which includes over 12,000 feet of climbing. I've climbed Mt. Ventoux and during our Vuelta trip a number of the famous cols of the Pyrenees. Since my first race 7 years ago, I have finished dozens of road races, criteriums and time trials and suffered up a number of hill climbs including two up Mt Evans, which ascends 7,000 feet over 27 miles and ends at a 14,223 foot elevation! In 2009 and 2010, I had competed in 65 cycling races finishing first and third respectively in the American Cycling Association's Best All Around Rider competition for 55+ women. Yes, I could do it.

When it came to doing RAAM, a nonstop 3,000 mile race, was going to be new territory. It was like a series of time trails, only doing them back to back to back for four hours and then repeating the sequence four hours later for a total of some 160 times during the course of a week. In fact, my mother's 2011 Christmas card which summarized her travels for the year included the postscript, "Amy is planning to do the Race Across America. I think she's awfully old to be undertaking a race like that".

A mother's cautionary instinct never ends. But her concern became more of an inducement than anything else. It couldn't possibly have deterred me. Besides, she had always been very active herself, had been an excellent tennis player when she was younger and was still playing play golf in her late 80's despite failing eyesight.

So age wasn't an issue. I compete against too many women that are my age and older, who are exceptional athletes, to see that as a limitation. So to me it was really a consideration of training and commitment, nothing more. Along with Mike's assurance, I grew to where I knew when I accepted a challenge that yes, I could "do it".

After eating and receiving a quick massage, I fell on the big bed in the back next to Dina to try and catch some sleep. But as we moved down the highway, every imperfection in the asphalt was magnified by the spring board effect that the rear of the RV experienced. When we hit a crack in the pavement, the small movement of the axle would be accentuated by the flexing floorboard underneath us, which, when releasing its energy, would fling us upward. And after momentarily experiencing weightlessness, we would crash back down on the bed to await the next launch. This constant movement made any sleep gained rather fitful.

In a best case scenario, a ride segment of 4 hours would cover 80 miles and there would be an hour and a half of driving in the RV before stopping at the next meeting place. With two teams splitting the riding chores, one would be off the bike for 12 hours each day. This would suggest that there should be enough time to get a decent amount of sleep.

But there were 6 changeovers every day, each of which included some eating and drinking, going to the bathroom, grabbing a sponge bath or, if lucky, a shower and getting a massage. Sometimes, RVs were routed on an alternate road not shared with racers making the distance longer. The one or two hours we had after reaching the next team exchange proved to be the best times for sleep, but the amount of deep sleep we would get was at risk. Deep sleep is necessary not only to help one remain alert while riding, but also this sleep sequence enables the body to push blood to the muscles for recovery and repair.

So combining all the variables, road noise, movement of the crew, bouncing in the air to each meeting point, waking up to get ready a half hour before changing teams, to say nothing about the difficulty of sleeping during daylight hours, our actual quality sleep time was perhaps 3 or 4 good hours a day. As the week wore on, the effects of not getting deep sleep were bound to increase.

Julie and Ann were already up the road and they would ride the next 89.3 miles to Glamis. There was a descent of 700 feet across the desert floor down to the edge of the Salton Sea at 227 feet below sea level and skirt the southern shore before reaching TS #2 in Brawley.

The Salton Sea occupies an area that was once part of the Gulf of Mexico, but over time, deposits from the Colorado River sealed it off and created a large, normally dry geological sink. It had filled with water in past eras, but in 1900 it was dry when the California Development Company began diverting Colorado River water to create the Imperial Valley agricultural area. Run-off from farming began to create a shallow lake, but in 1905, heavy silting of the irrigation ditch followed by massive flooding from torrential rains and up river snowmelt resulted in a flood that created a lake that was 35 miles long and 15 miles wide, which remains to this day. This mistake is fortunate for with the destruction of coastal wetlands, the Salton Sea has become migratory bird central for this part of the world.

There is another sink in California north of where we are now. It's called Death Valley, so named because of the deaths among members of the wagon train Juliet Brier traveled with so long ago. Their ill-advised short cut included a harrowing 20 mile traverse across the Valley floor. Although only one of her party died there, with the others perishing on the alkali flats of the Mojave Desert, the sink's hostile and barren environment earned it the name.

When we talk of the people who opened the west, we talk principally of men who found the trails, surveyed the routes and laid the tracks. But, you don't have to be 6'3" and bearded to prevail. Juliet's passage through this area was an extreme example of courage, and served as an inspiration to others in her group.

During her trek, Juliet and her children had to frequently walk ankle deep through shifting desert sands not unlike the conditions in the area around Glamis, our next vehicle meeting point. It is located in the heart of the Algodones Sand Dune country along the California Arizona border; the area de Anza stumbled into on his first try. This made pulling over on a shoulder to change riders at times a risky venture. RAAM Rules for follow vehicles required them to pull 5 feet off the road from the fog line on the right hand side. This was difficult in some places, impossible in others, so there was a constant need to make sure a good spot was located for each rider exchange. Nothing could be worse than having a van get stuck on the side of the road. The ability to support two riders and execute rolling exchanges would then become difficult.

Sure enough, 20 miles from Glamis, Joe pulled the Toyota off the highway to put Ann on the road and sank in deep enough so that the wheels just spun when he attempted to move. Gunning the engine and pushing it only made it worse. Fortunately, each follow vehicle had been equipped by Jack with an emergency kit which included a tow strap. A quick radio call to the other crew not far behind alerted them of the situation.

As Julie and the Audi approached, Joe jumped out, threw open the back hatch, rummaged around and grabbed the tow belt. He moved to the front, scooped away some sand, and looped it around the front suspension. Julie pulled in and Ann took off. The Audi, which had a sturdy bike carrier attached to a trailer hitch receptacle, backed up to the Toyota. Joe quickly wrapped the nylon belt around it, jumped back in behind the wheel. The Audi was able to pull the van out of the sand with no problem and the team didn't miss a beat. The LS&G crew was becoming proficient in extracting stuck vehicles

Not far from us, the German team got their RV stuck in the sand too, and George Thomas who was out on the course saw Joe freeing up the Toyota, stopped and asked if there might be some way we might help them. Sorry, not a chance. Joe didn't think our nylon tow straps were strong enough.

It was during Ann and Julie's first ride that we lost a large amount of time versus the Raw Milk Cats record. Santa Ana wind conditions pushed against them and made what should have been a fast segment slow in terms of speed. On the ride going into the Time Station in Brawley, they managed only 18.2 mph, while RMC had done that portion at a 25.4 mph average. When we passed through Brawley 8½ hours into the race, we were already 1:33 hours down on the record.

Groups that have done this race frequently, look at the first several days as a time when energy levels are high and seek to take advantage of a rider's fresh legs to really push hard. This desert section is typically where good speeds in the mid twenty miles per hour can be obtained. We did not have a specific race plan other than where to stop. Now, a big time gap to RMC so early in the race would be tough to overcome without some help from Mother Nature.

Chapter 10

Night Ride

"Amy, they're getting close. It's time to get ready". It was Mike's voice.

"What do you want to eat?" he continued.

I sat up in a dark fog trying to get a sense of where I was.

"Do you want some oatmeal and yogurt?" he asked.

"No. I don't know," I responded. I really didn't feel like eating anything. Nothing appealed to me.

"You've got to eat something. Let me toast a bagel." He offered.

"Okay", I managed.

Mike got my cooler together and made a peanut butter and jelly sandwich for me. Richie opened up the outside storage bins and retrieved a large bag of ice from one of the ice chests we had there.

As the other team came in, we would be told by the crew on the road who was riding, establishing which vehicle would come in first, and the rider assigned to that vehicle would be the first one out on the bike. It would be me. It was now 10:30 pm and it was still very warm in the 90's, The sky was clear with a small sliver of a waning moon giving limited visibility to the flat sandy terrain on either side of the road. A closed gas station was behind us and a mostly empty RV park across the road gave the place a ghost town's feel. The German Hubert Schwarz team's RV had escaped the sand in Glamis and had pulled off the road behind their riders who were up the road in front of us and soon they would move to overtake them and set up their next exchange point further on.

The Audi came in and Julie's bike was taken off. She got out of the car gave me a hello and headed toward the RV. This was pretty much the extent of the conversational interplay we would have throughout the race. My contact with Ann was even less. The brief moments we would have occurred when she finished and I started out at the team exchange points. This would be one of those times. I could see the lights of the Toyota behind Ann edging toward us. Richie and Paul were behind me in the Audi having taken over from the 2 Daves. The follow crews had changed with the riders at the first 2 meeting places. From here on out, they would change at every other turnover.

The section from there to Time Station 3 in Parker, Arizona was 61.4 miles. I threw a leg over my bike and clipped my right foot in and turned to look. Butterflies danced in my stomach. Ann came in put a foot down and I pushed off and after a half dozen strokes, got out of the saddle to gain speed and then settled in. It only took me 3 or 4 minutes to find a good rhythm and realize I was going to be okay.

We were heading north east and began a 12 mile steady 700 foot climb up the south side of Black Mountain. Behind me, the loud speaker on the Audi was playing some jarring heavy metal music. I circled my finger in the air, which was my signal to change the song and something more listenable came up. After 15 minutes of riding, I could see the flashing lights of the Toyota reflected by the surrounding desert sand. Dina was waiting. We were back in our groove.

It would be the first extended night ride for me. There was a belief that during training, we should experience some night time distance, to get used to it. Kathy put it on my training schedule. Ann would get up at 3 in the morning to ride. Dina did a 60 hour interval ride that mimicked the demands of the race, Julie got some night riding in. But, other than the 2 team practices, I hadn't done any.

And as it turned out, it wasn't an issue. I found that riding at night was pleasant. In fact, I concluded that it was preferable. I experienced a feeling of freedom. It was peaceful. There was less traffic, the sun was down, heat was less of an issue, and the winds usually would die down, although this would prove not always to be the case. Without much to see, other than the dark silhouettes of the terrain on either side of the road and a stretch of pavement illuminated by the headlights of the Audi, accentuated by a small but brighter circle thrown out from the LED light on my handlebars, I found myself in a contained environment.

Racers refer to being in a "hurt locker" when dealing with the physical pain of a hard climb or trying to maintain a high speed during a breakaway. I disappeared into my own "night locker" during the race. Each 15 to 20 minutes on the bike I would find my tempo and pedal away. The music over the Audi's loud speaker, the wind from my riding, occasional animal noises and passing cars were infrequent and failed to break the spell.

Safety rules required that nighttime exchanges were stationary rather than the rolling variety we executed during the day. Dina waited until I pulled in alongside and stopped. As I did, she pushed off, clicked into her pedals and began her turn. Each time out, I felt strong. I was fresh and my energy level was high. And as we traded pulls I would find a good solid tempo, and drill away into the looming night.

After cresting Black Mountain, it would be rolling to slightly downhill terrain for the next 20 miles. The road went straight through the arid, flat, featureless landscape. We had left the soft sands behind us and except for the scattered black outlines of low brushy vegetation, the land seemed bare. After several hours, we began to approach farm areas near the Colorado River that uses flood irrigation to grow heat resistant crops like alfalfa and cotton. As we got closer, the smell of vegetation became more apparent.

The route turned from an easterly direction toward the north. As it did, the head winds became less of a factor and despite the climbing our speed had increased to an average of 19.1 mph in the section ending in Blythe. It had taken us just over 3 hours, but RMC's girls were still flying at that point having averaged 22.4 mph. So at Blythe, we now had 235 miles behind us but had lost another 39 minutes to the record.

Dina and I clambered into the RV and dined on chicken and rice again. It will be 2 am before we get into our bed to try and grab a few hours of sleep. Ann and Julie (Team B) were now on the road and headed toward our next transition in Bouse, AZ, 26 miles past Time Station #4 in Parker. They would ride for 3 hours 48 minutes. The terrain was relatively flat with minimal elevation gain until Parker where the road began a gradual 400 foot rise to the next turnover. They would continue in a northerly direction along the west edge of the agricultural land that lies beside the Colorado River. Their average speed improved to above 20 mph for the first time, but it was still below the 21.1 mph achieved by RMC in that section. The differential was now at 2:22 hours.

Parker is located on the Colorado River and is named for General Ely Parker, a Seneca Indian, who rose to the rank of General and served as an aide to General Grant during the Civil War. He was also made the first Director of the Bureau of Indian Affairs. Although he studied to be a lawyer as a young man, he wasn't allowed to take the bar exam because Indians were not given status as American Citizens at the time.

Once through the town, the race route leaves the fertile lands along the river and turns south on Arizona State Hwy 72 through a flat desert landscape relatively empty save for drought tolerant creosote bushes. The road is two lanes with narrow shoulders. The road turns east after a dozen miles or so then veers southeast towards Bouse. This is a small little highway town that survived its beginnings as a mining camp and now is a community of vacation homes.

Chapter 11

Transition Zone

Bouse is also the site of an ancient Indian Geoglyph called "The Fisherman", which represents a man spearing fish carved in the earth which some believe was made 2,000 years ago. It is one of the 200 Blythe geoglyphs that can be found in the lower Colorado Basin the largest of which is 17 feet long. They weren't discovered until 1923 when a pilot in a low flying plane passed over and noticed them. It was the following year in 1924, that Native Americans were granted United States citizenship. This was a little too late for Ely.

We're now in the northeastern part of the Sonoran Desert, in the bench lands that are the transition zone between the Colorado River Basin and higher elevations of the Colorado Plateau. It will be a zone we will have to pass through to leave behind the unrelenting sun and heat of the desert to reach the more moderate temperatures of the higher mountains.

The SuperNova has stopped next to the Desert Pueblo RV Resort and we began to replenish our supply of water and ice, a requirement that the heat we were dealing with would require throughout the rest of the trip.

Dina and I were up as the sky began to lighten. After some granola and a cream cheese and jelly slathered bagel, Mike helped me fill several water jugs and a big zip lock bag full of ice, plus the standard peanut butter and jelly sandwich along with other snacks for our next leg, which would end in Congress – Time Station # 6 – 84 miles away. It was 5:00 am local time when Julie came in. Dina was first on the bike. Mike had secured mine to the rear rack and I walked to the Audi to get in. I could already feel the heat of the early sun on my skin as it began its trek through the sky driving the temperature to a high of 114° F that day.

Once on the road, Route 72 narrowed to a point where there were no shoulders and the surface was old, pitted, rough pavement. We passed through what seemed flat unchanging desert, but were in the process of gaining 2,200 feet in elevation that morning. At 23 miles we hit the town of Hope, which consisted of a small church at the junction with US 60 and a nearby RV Park. Leaving town a sign beside the highway told us "Your (sic) Now Beyond Hope". Not the message I was looking for. Perhaps someone knew what was in store for us that day.

At mile 30, we would pass Time Station #5 in Salome. We were doing 5 mile pulls and each time out I felt the sun press down a little more. Each time back in the car, I felt my skin relax in the coolness.

The highway is now paralleling the course of the Centennial Wash, which looks dry as a bone, but has apparently flooded a couple of times in the last decade. There is obviously water here because orchards and truck farm fields can be seen on either side of the road. When we reach Aquila, the town sign boasts its world famous melons. To the east, staring down at us is Eagle Eye Peak a jagged looking mountain with a hole near the summit that goes all the way through.

Back out on the bike again, the sun is climbing higher in the sky and it feels like the heat is pressing down more intensely than it had during the ride before. As a mental game, I began to envision things that would cool me off. Out on the bike in front of the Audi with some rock song playing on the speaker, it occurred to me that what I desired most on a hot summer day as a young girl growing up in Illinois farm country was to go down to Lee's Variety Store, lean into the cool display case and take out a fudgesicle. I would take off the paper wrapper and watch cold vapors rising from it that looked like smoke. Then as I walked home in the heat, the pleasure of putting it in my mouth and biting into it was indescribable. It seemed to cool me off all over. As I pedaled along up the long grade, I began to fixate on it. I began to visualize it and taste the texture in my mouth.

When I returned to the Audi, I began to talk about it. "Boy would a fudgesicle taste good right now"

I must have talked about it on several occasions because finally, one of the Dave's in my support crew in a radio conversation with the RV giving them our estimated arrival time, said, "Oh, one more thing, Amy wants a fudgesicle.....make sure she gets it when she finishes!"

Climbing in the heat and combating headwinds remained a problem and our average speed dipped as the run to Salome TS #5 was at 16.9 mph and from there to Congress 16.4 mph. The competition was above 19 mph in this section and by TS #6 we're 3:30 down.

Congress, AZ – 395 miles – 0:22:17

Dina had taken the final pull into Congress and I had gotten out of the Audi and planned to wait for her to finish and ask how she was handling the heat. Mike came up behind me and pressed something cold on the back of my neck. I turned and there it was in its gaily colored paper wrapper, a fudgesicle. It couldn't have been better.

As Dina came in, Julie started out on her ride with the Audi falling in behind. Joe drove in and pulled the Toyota into the parking area and Ann climbed in while Tyson put her bike in the car rack.

Before starting back out, Joe got out of the car waving an insulated cup over his head and walked to where Mike and I and several other crew members were standing

"I need coffee" he announced to no one in particular.

Mike took his cup from him and headed to a hospitality tent to fill it up. At the same time, Jack ran into an adjacent grocery store and bought a large Styrofoam cup filled to the brim.

While he was waiting, Joe noticed me standing there and as an apparent explanation as to why he needed coffee, he stated importantly, "I've got to get the girls up the hill".

He seemed taken with the importance of his responsibilities. I was fully aware of who he was and what he was doing. Dina and I were in this game too. We had been going up hills. No one had been grandly announcing our upcoming destination. Maybe, I was being too sensitive or too analytical. I concluded that I just had to channel Juliet's perseverance, focus on my contribution and keep turning my pedals over toward Annapolis.

The Congress Time Station has a reputation as being a racer favorite because the Bullshifter's Bicycle Club from Phoenix sets up a hospitality station every year with coffee, ice water, fruit and snacks for racers and crew. However, the big draw is an above ground pool filled with cool water.

In fact, Dina was aware of its existence and used the vision of diving in a cool swimming pool to keep her going, just as I had envisioned the icy, chocolaty taste of a fudgesicle. As the sun climbed higher in the sky, she kept telling herself that she was getting closer to the pool. Although, she thought it was a regular in ground pool at a motel and couldn't understand why the owner would allow a bunch of sweaty, dirty cyclists to jump in clothes and all.

We arrived at 10:17 local time and the 100+ degree temperature lured us toward it. It was 3 or 4 feet high and about 10 feet in circumference. But it was clear, surprisingly cool, and had rippling water on the surface. I jumped in, shorts, jersey and all and received a souvenir rubber ducky for hitting bottom from one of the club members there. It was a great way to get refreshed, wash off the road grime and clean my shirt and shorts at the same time. Dina followed me in and Mike took the opportunity to strip down to his shorts and climb in as well. Joe had shuddered at the thought of climbing into a pool where a bunch of other sweaty racers and grimy crew had splashed about before, but it hit the spot for me.

This along with savoring my icy fudge bar after hours spent in the hot sun riding on a bike was blissful to say the least. And as I would soon find out, it was the best thing I was going to get that day.

From Congress to Prescott, Team B would only cover 46 miles and do it in 3:02. This stretch started with the Yarnell Grade and involved 1,800 feet of climbing in the first 9 miles. Then a little over half way they would have another 2,800 feet over a distance of 13 miles. A tough ride in the middle of a scorching day for sure.

They averaged 16.4 mph in that stretch reaching Prescott at 1:30 pm in the afternoon. While this schedule limited their time in the sun during the hottest part of the day, this meant not much recovery time for Dina and me. We would be back out on the road in the heat with a short turn around for what would prove to be, time-wise, the longest segment of race so far.

When the RV reached Prescott, we ran into Steve Medcroft, the US distributor of Santini USA. His office is located near Phoenix, some 110 miles to the south and I was pleased that he made the trip up to see us and cheer us on. Steve had been a reporter with Velo News, a magazine devoted to serious cyclists and racers, several years before and had covered RAAM in 2003. That was the year that Brett Malin, a member of the 4 man Vail Go-Fast team was killed by a tractor trailer near Pie Town, NM, an incident that Steve covered. Brett had just finished a 30 minute leg and did a U-turn to go back to his support vehicle when the truck came over a rise in the highway just ahead of him. They both tried to avoid one another, but turned in the same direction.

Brett's death was tragic, but the Vail team returned the following year and rode in the memory of their fallen team mate. In the latter part of that race, they were riding head to head with two other teams when they lost a rider to an injury in West Virginia and ended up finishing 2 hours behind the winners. This year's race included a team from Slovenia riding in memory of Jure Robic, a former men's solo winner, who had died after being hit by a motorist in his home country.

Using the physical demands of the race as a demonstration of one's respect for the sacrifices of others and overcoming the adversity that the race entails makes a powerful statement to those on the outside and to those of us racing. This display stays with you. And I think this made a lasting impression on Steve and perhaps was helpful in his development of an interest in getting Santini to support LS&G's RAAM effort.

Whatever the reason for his generosity, the kits were very much appreciated – and with Tasso's design work– I thought the most stylish on the road that year.

There was another link to the uniform story. Steve wouldn't have become involved were it not for Rob Brown, a Denver based bike and ski rep. He had directed me to Steve as he knew they were pushing to expand in the U.S. and had a new women's chamois design for which they wanted exposure. So our team was fortunate to have friendships and support from the cycling industry and in Steve's case, someone who also took the time out to show support and give us a wave as we pulled out of Prescott that torrid afternoon to begin our dramatic ride to Flagstaff. It didn't hurt that the NBC News film crew were with us that day adding to the buzz.

So a few minutes after chatting with Steve and introducing him to Mike and some of the crew, the Toyota pulled into the Wal-Mart

Supercenter mall where we had parked the RV. We wheeled out to the far side of the highway that Julie would be coming in on. The bicycles would be exchanged. Dina would start out and our caravan would continue eastward

Prescott, AZ – 441.12 miles 1 day 1:19 hours

Chapter 12

Black Mesa

Our ride from Prescott was the penultimate segment of the "death zone', which fully lived up to its reputation for tough climbing and intense heat.   It eliminated the three 2 person relay teams doing RAW and a clutch of soloists that had started earlier in the week. Most had not made it past Cottonwood. But Dina and I made it through and with Hayman and Oak Creek Canyons and Flagstaff behind; we luxuriated in nearly 5 hours of well-deserved rest and recovery time before we would be back on the road.

In turn, Team B put their time off the bike to good use, covering the distance from Flagstaff to Tonalea at a decent speed and passed through the Time Station at Tuba City with a 20 mph average, taking time back from RMC. Tuba City was founded by Mormons in 1872 and named in honor of the Hopi chief Tuuvi who converted to their religion. They had been sent out by Brigham Young to colonize the nether parts of the Great Basin and to capitalize on the many natural springs in the area for agriculture. But they didn't last. Chester Arthur designated the area as a reservation in the 1880's, and by 1903, the Navajos had replaced the Mormons.

The RV had a straight shot to our changeover spot, so we had several hours of good sleep on the side of the road before being roused just before midnight. The elevation was 5,400 feet allowing the temperature to cool into the 70's. We had a crew change there. My guys, Richie and Paul would be replaced by the 2 Dave's. The retiring crew had just put in 11 hours during the two 95 mile segments, which put them at the edge of their endurance. Fortunately, the traffic was minimal with only one turn since leaving Flagstaff

After wolfing down some granola and yogurt, I went outside where Mike had rolled out my bike. We waited next to a gas station at an intersection in the middle of wide open rangeland. The night was dark, but the overhead sky was dotted with thousands of visible stars. I could see the shapes of mobile homes and a few lights in the distance. Scattered barks and yelps from neighborhood dogs punctuated the quiet.

I would be the first out on the bike. As I waited for Ann's arrival, the sounds of the crew moving around, crunching gravel under their feet, talking on the radio and relaying location information seemed amplified. Then the car lights of the Toyota appeared on the horizon, seemingly stationary at first, then gradually getting closer. Several minutes passed before Ann's shadow could be seen bobbing on her pedals in front of the van. Finally, the sound of music over the speaker became audible as she closed the last several hundred meters, came along side me and stopped. It's my turn now and I pushed off and pedaled out into the night, dragging the Audi behind.

Each time, before I began my first pull, I would feel apprehensive. No matter how many times I would do this, it would hit me. But each time I got the bike moving and settled into my tempo, those fears would go away.

The road was straight with a good shoulder, the pavement smooth, although a rumble strip inside the fog line was an annoyance when I sometimes wandered onto it. Our route would take us north east on the Navajo Trail near Hopi Indian lands. Several miles into my ride, I could just make out in the dark two odd looking narrow buttes that rise some 40 feet in the air. I found out later they are aptly named The Elephant Feet. Then the road swung slightly north into the narrow canyon of Laguna Wash with the dark shape of Black Mesa to the north. To the south were Third Mesa, and the Hopi pueblo of Oraibi. Established before 1100 AD, it is the oldest continuously occupied city in North America. When the early Anasazi Indian cultures left their cliff dwellings because of drought, this is one of the places where they emigrated. Although much in ruins, a section is still lived in by several Hopi clans who cling to a traditional lifestyle by resisting modern ways, which includes forbidding anyone to take photographs of their dwellings.

Through these sacred Indian lands, we started with a gradual 1,300 feet of uphill for the first 30 miles and from there trending downhill to Kayenta. About 10 miles into the ride, we returned to the Navajo Indian reservation and passed by a sign for Cow Springs; I could see a sprinkling of mobile homes some distance back from the road.

At Cow Springs, we had traveled 640 miles. Mike pointed this out to me because it equaled the distance that Ann, Julie and I had covered, competing in the Karen Hornbostel Cherry Creek Time Trial series earlier in April and May.

This race series consisted of a 9.6 miles time trial on Wednesday afternoon for seven weeks. In their generosity, the organizers had donated 4 starting slots to the 3 of us to give us a race experience not unlike what we would face during RAAM. The course was on rolling terrain that included two punchy climbs requiring some out of the saddle efforts to maintain speed.

Each race took 24 to 29 minutes depending on the racer. Then we would have about 20 minutes between each race for recovery, which gave us a good way to sample the physical demands of repetitive hard efforts with short rests in between.

We rode 67 races which added up to combined total of 643.2 miles at an average speed of 21.8 mph. If we could have ridden at that speed, we would have been 5 hours ahead of RMC by now.

Ann was the fastest and registered the most consistent times finishing with an average speed of 22.9 mph, Julie was next at 21.8 mph and my average was 20.2 mph. What was encouraging about my performance was that I had a notable improvement from the first to last race of two minutes for my average finishing time and I ended up clocking a 21.5 mph average during the last 4 race session we did.

I had a further test of that on the weekend before we left for Oceanside. Mike and I raced in a 10 km Time Trial at the Rocky Mountain Senior Games. We had done this race several years before so the time trial would give me a further indication of whether I was getting any faster. I finished in 16:41, which lowered my best time by 1:32 minutes. And I was not a heck of a lot slower than Mike's time that day. I ended up winning that race and a 20 km road race that followed. These results had been a further indication that I was rounding into good shape for RAAM.

After Cow Springs we continued climbing through the dark landscape up something called Tsegi Canyon. I can make out mesas and other smooth mountain shapes against the night sky. The climbing ended at Marsh Pass and then began a gradual descent down a flat valley which was the product of Laguna Creek.

I finished our leg with a ride into the village of Kayenta. It is a trading post that was a way point on the Old Spanish Trail that Antonio Armijo established in 1829 opening trade between Santa Fe and Los Angeles. It is now a tourist destination and boasts a Burger King that houses the Navajo WW II Code Talker Museum.

Just past the Burger King there was an intersection. The loud speaker told me to make a left turn where I saw the RV with Ann waiting in front. I pulled up alongside and Ann stepped up on her pedal and pushed down. The Toyota pulled out behind her. I saw the blinking yellow lights move away in my periphery and in moments they were gone. We had completed the 49 mile ride in 2:42 hours equaling RMC's 19 mph speed for this section. It was now 4 a.m. MST and the faint beginning of dawn lightened the eastern horizon.

Kayenta 679.8 miles 1 day 14:42 hours

Team B were back on for the next 84.3 miles. Their route swung north, through dramatic buttes and peaks of Monument Valley and on into Utah. We would now be on Mountain Time. There would be relatively little elevation change, with the first 44 miles to Mexican Hat flat to downhill. They took advantage of the descent and a favorable tailwind to average 23.5 mph in this section. The final 40 miles had rolling hills with a short 800 foot climb between mile 50 and 60 and here their speed would drop to 17 mph. They would finish in Montezuma Creek in 4:13 hours.

We would shortly be leaving the reservation of the Navajo or Diné, a people who had their own excursion across America. They were a proud but aggressive tribe and had a history of fighting with other Indians, the Spanish and the newly arrived Americans. In 1863, Kit Carson, under orders from General Carleton rounded up and drove them from this area on the Long March to the infamous Bosque Redondo on the Pecos River in New Mexico.

Upwards of 12,000 Navajo were uprooted over a period of several years and forced to move there. Thousands died on the way and others died of disease and malnutrition after arriving. However, in recognition of its mismanagement, in 1868, the U.S. eventually allowed the Navajo to return to their homelands back up the same route in a mass of humanity that was said to be 10 miles long. Of all the marches native peoples made in the 1800's, this was the only one that allowed the Indians to return to their ancestral home. To this day, the journey they undertook is said to define a Navajo's personhood.

I expect the journey we are on, while under decidedly more benign circumstances will leave a lasting impression on us.

Chapter 13

Sutcliffe Winery to Wolf Creek

It was now 8 am Mountain Time. With hot tea and a bagel in my stomach, I climbed out of the RV and took in the surroundings. Montezuma Creek is named for a small stream that feeds the San Juan River alongside of which we are now traveling. Mormons also tried to settle here and farm, but it too is now principally a Navajo community, still within reservation lands.

Dina and I would be back on for a 67 mile leg to Mancos. We started in the relatively flat lands of southern Utah that features scrubby vegetation covering the reddish soil with low bluffs and buttes on the horizon. We followed the course of the San Juan River, which cut through the red sandstone in several places creating smooth flat surfaces. But after 16 miles along Route 162 we turned onto the Ismay Trading Post Road.

I took over for Dina there as we entered a valley carved by another San Juan tributary, McElmo Creek. Next to the freedom I felt riding at night, early morning was second best. The temperature was cool, the air refreshing and my legs usually felt good. The road tipped up and we climbed above the valley floor on the Ismay road going straight as the creek followed a horseshoe bend to the south. After a mile the road crested and started back downhill. We entered irrigated farmland and I began to see green fruit orchards and rows of grape vines on the valley floor. After 2 days of desert scenery, it was a treat to be riding in the greenness of McElmo Canyon as the road crisscrossed the bubbling creek several times.

Dina was on the bike when we entered Colorado. We had left Navajo lands and were now in Ute territory. We were also entering the "Land of the Ancients" south of the cliff dwellings of Hovenweep and given the water supply, an area the early occupants farmed. People who live here say that it is not uncommon to look down and pick up a piece of pottery off the ground left behind over 1,000 years ago.

We passed Sutcliffe Vineyards, with its Tuscan inspired main house. It is farmed by John Sutcliffe, a delightful Welshman who is unique for this part of the country. Mike and I had visited Sutcliffe in the past and consider it as our favorite Colorado winery. I was on familiar territory, near my stomping grounds and on roads that I had ridden before. It felt good to be there.

We would climb some 2,800 feet passing through Cortez, an early Western town established in the 1880's to house workers who blasted tunnels and built irrigation canals to channel water from the Dolores River, to the flat but arid Montezuma Valley. Here we turned due east toward the next vehicle meeting point in Mancos, which we reached after 4 hours of riding.

Mancos was named in 1776 by the Spanish explorer Escalante. His route had gone through rocky scree when crossing the mountains and mangled the horses feet, thus generating the name. The town was an early commercial center, after the enactment of the San Juan Cession of 1873, which enabled the U.S. to take back a huge piece of the Ute Indian Reservation created just 10 years prior. The Utes, originally, had been given a reservation consisting of the western third of Colorado, which at one time was considered uninhabitable by Europeans. But when gold and silver was found in Telluride and Silverton it was concluded that perhaps it was habitable after all and anyway the reservation area was too generous. So a big piece was taken back to provide access to the mines.

Mancos became a boom town back then, but it is now a small sleepy village that serves as an entryway to the cliff dwellings of the Mesa Verde National Park. In the end, the Utes ended up with a handful of small reservations, in Colorado, Utah and New Mexico; although these lands included the rich San Juan Basin shale gas play making the Southern Utes, one of the richest in America.

We changed teams there and Julie and Ann would now be on a 64 mile leg paralleling the Animas River which would include a 1,500 foot climb up Hesperus Pass near Baldy Mountain before descending into Chimney Rock to finish their leg in 3:20.

It was about here that John Marchetti posted...

"Ann just whooped ass on Hesperus Pass! It was Beautiful, a T800 racer passed Ann on a downhill and anyone who knows Ann, knows she wasn't going to let them take it away for long. On the next climb she started to overtake him and he stood up. Ann stayed in the saddle and kept pulling away from him..... Just as sweet as you please".

Ann can climb. She is good.

Before Chimney Rock, they passed through the Time Station in Durango at 2 days and 19 minutes. We were now 3:14 hours behind RMCs record time. We were also 2 hours behind the finishing time of the Denver Spokes RAW team of 2 years before.

It was our turn again and at 3:30 pm MDT, we started out of the rest area near Navajo Lake Road that leads to Chimney Rock. We could see to the south two towering rock formations that rise from a ridgeline, one of which was very straight and narrow and square on top, thus giving the area its name. There was also the site of an early Pueblo Kiva near the ridgeline. We are now in pinion pine and grassland country at nearly 7,000 feet. It is dry and warm. Good cycling weather.

Julie and Ann had blistered the downhill off of Baldy and we maintained a good rate of speed, because by the time we had climbed to Pagosa Springs we had clawed back 1:13 hours of the time deficit we were down to RMC when we had reached Flagstaff and we had pulled ahead of the T800, Above + Beyond Cancer team and had passed the Equipe Schwarz German men's team that had started ahead of us in Oceanside.

Pagosa is the Ute Indian word for healing waters and the area boasts one of the largest and hottest mineral springs in the world. I had been here before and can attest to the hot part of the claim. I would have enjoyed, a nice muscle relaxing soak right then and there, but such was not in the cards.

We were now riding into the San Juan Range of the Rockies. We were making good time along the flats near the San Juan River on HWY 160, passing well-tended pastures and ranch land surrounded by pine woods. About 20 miles outside of Pagosa, we passed a sign announcing "Summit 8 miles, and began to head up a 7% grade to the 10,866 foot elevation of Wolf Creek Pass. We shorten our pulls to 3 miles, and the cool of the late afternoon helped me maintain a good rhythm.

Once over the summit we could see the Wolf Creek ski area, which averages a whopping 465 inches of snowfall annually. John Fremont found out the hard way how much it snows in the area when during his ill-advised expedition to establish an all-weather rail route to the west, he lost 10 men and 50 mules who succumbed to the cold and deep snows. All weather route?

It was also at Wolf Creek Pass that Shannon Gillespie, the heat stroke rider of Mucho Gusto climbed back on his bike for the first time since was stricken in Arizona. His team had struggled since having the second rider calamity – mistaking a Clorox disinfecting wipe for a less painful Wet Wipe. This took their best climber out of the rider rotation at a time when he was needed most.

So for a half day with Shannon out, they had been reduced to 3 riders and with the Clorox episode were further whittled to just 2 cyclists. After a rest in Durango to gather strength, they tackled the Baldy Mountain climb into Pagosa Springs, followed by the ascent to the summit of Wolf Creek Pass.

By then, the nausea that Shannon had experienced had passed and while still a little wobbly in the knees he took over.

"They put me in the saddle and kind of duct taped me back on the bike," he recounted in their race video. "Then they pushed me over the edge and got me back into it. The fresh air in my face really helped. It was mostly downhill from there and I was able to keep going for 5 hours."

The descent starts with a long 6% grade and it was 66 miles in all of downhill from there to Alamosa and while everyone else slept Shannon relied on gravity and what strength he could muster to hang on down the mountain and across the flats towards Kansas.

We didn't go that far, after crossing the Pass at the Continental Divide, we began a 2,800 foot, 17 mile descent to South Fork where we would change crews. After the summit, the road passed under avalanche sheds, then swung north past forests of ponderosa, bristlecone and limber pine as it followed the South Branch of the Rio Grande River down into the San Luis Valley.

We completed the 66 miles in just over 4 hours. Our speed from Pagosa was only 15.4 mph but given that we had matched the speed of RMC in that stretch and for a period of time pulled ahead of the German Equipe Schwarz team, it was a good effort.

Chapter 14

Tobin Country

From South Fork, the road continued to drop and then flatten out as we left the San Juan's for Julie and Ann's 70 mile leg to Fort Garland. They took advantage of a gathering tailwind and the downslope to average 25.2 mph in the 46 mile segment to Alamosa, our fastest speed so far and a pace that equaled that of RMC. We were now one-third of the way to Annapolis at the 1,000 mile mark in 2 days and 8 hours. This put us exactly at a 7 day finishing - time schedule.

Alamosa – 2 days 8:05 hrs. – 1,006.3 miles

It was 10:30 pm when they reached Ft. Garland. Dina would be the first to ride. We were at 8,000 feet, it was cool and we made sure we had our jackets and leg warmers. This was to be a 78 mile effort and involved climbing two mountain passes our second such challenge in the last 2 days. When riding with the 2 Daves, I had made comments about a better balance in the load between the two squads, but there didn't seem to be any response. All I got was a blank stare. It was like talking to a wall.

Well okay, I finally concluded, you've come to the right people to handle this. I knew Dina was a horse, an exceptional endurance athlete, and she could do it. And me, I proved to myself that I could handle what came my way.

We're now in Tom Tobin's country. He was an early frontiersman who headed out on the Santa Fe Trail at age 13, was a cohort of Kit Carson, and served with Fremont and Kearney. He was one of 2 survivors of the massacre at Turley's Mill in 1846 and participated in the subsequent Battle of Taos Pueblo. But he was best known as the man who brought Felipe Espinosa to justice.

Felipe was said to have had a vision from the Virgin Mary to kill 100 Anglos for each one of the 6 family members he lost in the Mexican American War. He also claimed a land grant for Conejos County, where we are now riding. Kearney had defeated the Mexicans in this area and the U.S. had annexed the San Luis Valley along with New Mexico thus denying him his grant.

To drive the gringos out, Felipe and kin went on a killing spree against the newly arrived farmers and miners. They had dispatched 32 poor souls and had foiled several capture attempts, when the commander of Fort Garland finally sent for Tom Tobin to track him down. He gave him a squad of 16 cavalry soldiers to help, but Tom thought they were too noisy and slipped out of camp on his own. He then tracked the Espinosa's down, shot them and cut off their heads to prove it.

Tom lived a colorful life. His mother was half Cherokee, half African American and his father an Irish trapper. He married the daughter of a prominent Spanish family who settled in the area in the 1500's and survived a gun fight with his son-in-law Chris Carson, Kit's son. He was a dog lover who collected strays and when he died, dogs all over the valley were said to have all begun to howl at once in mourning.

No howling dogs tonight as we started out, just a howling tailwind heading north east toward La Veta Pass which cuts through the Sangre de Cristo Mountains. This was the site of Espinosa's last attempt at an attack on a wagonload of settlers. They got away and alerted the authorities, which helped Tom figure out where to track them down.

One mile out, we started climbing until we hit a false summit after 8 miles. After a short descent, the road turned up again as the grade gradually increased to 6%. We raised the summit 20 miles out of Ft. Garland at 9,418 feet which was followed by a 14 mile descent into the town of La Veta. Despite the climbing, we averaged a combined 18.3 mph between Alamosa and La Veta nearly equal to that of RMC. We now turned southwest for the climb up Cucharas Pass.

The earlier tailwind was now more in our face and we were being buffeted by gusts up to 30 mph forcing us to grind away in our lowest gears. The road had a 6% grade and rose 3,000 feet to the 9,941 foot summit. There is something other worldly about pedaling up a mountain in the dead of night, silhouetted by the headlights of the follow van. There were no other cars on the road and when I hit switchbacks mid-way up the north side near Deadman's Creek, the music blared behind me as I moved east, but when I swung west all I could hear was the wind. Two deer scampered across the road in front of me. It was pitch black outside of the area lit by the head lights.

As I came around the next turn, I was startled by noises from the darkness off to the left. Frightened, high pitched screeches made it sound like something was being killed. Unable to see anything, I assumed the worst, that a coyote or a mountain lion was killing a prey; possibly farm animals from the look of the area. It was eerie, and the hair on the back of my neck stood up as I now pedaled with more urgency.

Up ahead, Dina was waiting to take over. She had heard the sounds too and it gave her a scare as well. She had images of zombies or some other horror movie creature crashing through the brush. (Could it be the headless Espinosa seeking revenge?) Dina could see me in the distance, slowly coming up the grade. The noises began to move ahead of me toward where she waited. She was alarmed as well. All she could think of was for me to hurry. When I reached her, she took off, pedaling in earnest. Finally, the mysterious creatures stopped running and began braying. They were donkeys, who mut have been spooked by our presence. The ghost of Espinosa turned out to be just a few donkeys.

A lot of RAAM racing is repetitive. And while initially unsettling, a diversion such as the 'Espinosa Donkey Scare' on Cucharas Pass helped to keep one alert, add a shot of adrenalin and take the sting out of the legs during the climb.

Dina did the last part to the summit, where I took over again near Monument Lake. Initially it was flat, but it swung back in an easterly direction and then started down the flanks of the Spanish Peaks. This type of terrain is typically not my strong suit. I tend to be cautious on descents. But the easterly direction of the road put me back in a tail wind.

It was like being in a cocoon because riding with the wind limits the noise it makes. With big sweeping curves and a 2,000 foot descent ahead of us into Weston, I released the brakes and let the bike run. Afterwards, Richie told Mike I had hit 56 mph on the way down. Mike was amazed. He's not as bothered by high speed when going down-hill as much as I am, but anything near 50 mph for him is territory for white knuckle fear.

Descending this side of the pass is where Dr. Bob Breedlove an experienced RAAM soloist veered into an oncoming pick-up truck and was killed the year Much Gusto raced. The race can be unforgiving for rider inattention or error. Of this I was aware. Yet coming down the road, I felt alive with energy and self-confidence and let it fly.

My ride that night ranked as one of the more memorable I experienced during RAAM; right up there with my recovery mid-ride in the coolness of Oak Creek Canyon. When I had finished Cucharas and thought about the three passes that I had ridden that day, I knew that I could do this race, I knew that I could finish

RAAM. I had now survived the death zone and had conquered the Rockies. We were now headed toward easier terrain on the Great Plains and I assumed that the toughest parts were over. Whether I was right or not remained to be seen, but at that moment, I believed I had achieved a victory. I have promised myself to go back and ride Cucharas again. This time in daylight.

From the summit, it was another 26 miles to Weston our next exchange point. We reached it at 3:30 am MDT for a ride of just over 5 hours; our fourth such leg in the first 2 ½ days.

Dina was on the last run into Weston and I arrived first in the Audi. Mike was waiting for me and gave me a hug. He had been concerned about how I was holding up given our share of the load so far, and had been awake walking up and down the highway and looking in the direction I was coming from. His concerns were unnecessary. I was ecstatic. Dina rolled in and Julie pushed off. Michelle had been busy trying to organize a delivery of food that had been brought down from Denver so Mike warmed up some lasagna, which I picked at before climbing into bed.

The B Team would continue down the Purgatoire River through Trinidad and across the Arkansas River flood plain toward Kansas. Trinidad played a small role in the old West. It was a boom town on the southern supply route to Denver and benefitted from the discovery of gold in the nearby Spanish Peaks. Bat Masterson was the marshal here for a short period after his Dodge City days before moving to Denver to run gambling saloons. Despite a dangerous life in the old West, Bat was an old man when he died of a heart attack in New York City, while writing a newspaper column for the Morning Telegraph.

From Weston to Kim, the last stop in Colorado, it was a 93 mile flat to downhill run. The favorable winds continued to hold and pushed their speed to an average of 20.8 mph between Trinidad and Kim finishing in 4:30 hrs. This bettered the RMC pace. Over the last 12 Time Stations, we've beaten them 5 times and were even with them in all but 3 of the rest. We're hitting our stride.

Chapter 15

Prairie Winds

At Kim, Colorado, it's Dina and me again. As our prize for climbing 3 passes the prior day, we have been awarded the longest leg that the team will encounter during the entire race. It's a total of 100.3 miles. Despite the race's demands, I woke up at 7:30 am feeling reasonably refreshed. I had gotten a good sleep after the prior night's ride putting me more in sync with my normal circadian rhythm pattern. The first ride of the day was usually a good one and today would be no exception. While we're out on the plains, we're still at 5,700 feet and the temperature is moderate.

I eat a bagel that Mike had toasted with cream cheese and jelly along with a small bowl of granola. You would think I would be ravenous, but I seem to prefer taking on small amounts of food each time I eat, but I am eating constantly. We ride three times a day, and eat something before and after we ride and snack in the car between pulls.

Riders need to consume 6,000 calories a day. While I continue to add an energy and electrolyte mix to my water, I find that some of the performance gels, energy bars and the like are hard to get interested in. Regular food products are more fulfilling. There is something satisfying with biting down and crunching into a salty potato chip. The taste is better, the mouth-feel more pleasant, which makes it a lot easier to load the carbs. Snack food producers have my number. I have succumbed to yet another product, which I've added to my food bag; Ritz crackers with peanut butter. There's no hope for me.

Kim sits on Colorado's Eastern Plain. It's a small town with a couple of streets, some shade trees and a handful of farm service businesses and residences. We have been heading due east on US 160 which rolls through pancake flat rangeland and farming country. The road inexplicably makes a 90 degree turn to the north before reaching town, then turns 90 degrees a mile past it heading east again, arrow straight towards Kansas.

The town is also in the middle of the Comanche National Grasslands. This area and lands in the surrounding 4 states were once home to the dozen or so bands of the Comanche. This tribe owes its existence to European settlement. They grew rapidly as a separate Nation when several bands of Utes, Shoshone and others obtained horses after the Pueblo revolt in 1609 that temporarily drove the Spanish out of New Mexico. By the mid 1800's, they had developed a strong buffalo hunting horse culture that numbered 20,000. By the time their Chief, Quanah Parker surrendered and led them to the Ft. Sill Reservation in 1875, there were 1,600 left.

Quanah's mother was Cynthia Ann Parker, who had been kidnapped by the Comanche's at the age of 9 and subsequently married Chief Nocona. After 24 years with the Indians, she was rescued by Texas Rangers, but never readjusted to living with white culture. Heartbroken, she once tried to rejoin her tribal family but was caught and returned. Eventually, she stopped eating and died during an influenza outbreak. John Ford made a classic movie with John Wayne about it called "The Searchers". Cynthia's desire to return to her Indian family was a reaction seen from other kidnapped women and children during the settlement of the West. Home life for settler's wives in those days must have been pretty hard.

The wind that had pushed me down the east side of the Sangre de Cristo's and carried Julie and Ann to Kim was still in our favor. It was still coming out of the west and wWe would be riding in front of it, dead down wind. At the same time, we would enjoy a 2,400 foot loss in elevation. It would be our first major downhill without earning it with a climb so far in the race.

Tyson took Dina's time trial bike off the rack. He added air to the tires and quickly ran through the gears. But there was only one combination that mattered this morning; the biggest ring and the smallest cog. It was time for some speed.

I didn't bring mine as I had opted to bring a second road bike for my spare, even though Mike tried to convince me otherwise. I felt that riding tucked into my aero bars was giving me most of the benefits I would get from a time trial bike, and, if I had developed a problem with my first bike, I didn't want to get stuck riding a TT bike in the mountains, the geometry and the stiff frame made the ride too uncomfortable.

In fact, Julie had just experienced a problem with her primary road bike. She was having shifting problems. Tyson adjusted the cable tension, but that hadn't worked. He then determined that there was an issue with the bottom bracket, so he pulled her crank assembly out to work on it and had inadvertently left the left crank sitting on the back bumper of the RV when it pulled out. Needless to say, the crank wasn't there when we pulled into the next exchange point. Julie fortunately, had a back-up road bike and was in good shape. I made sure Mike was aware of this because for me, it justified my decision.

Dina is out first. It is 8:01 am, so it's a rolling start. Once Julie passes her, she headed north for a mile, then turned east with the Toyota right behind. Cue the background music. There is not a single geographic variation on the horizon. There is nothing to slow the winds coming out of the west. Dina dropped her head down and dug in.

I was up the road waiting to take over. Normally, I start out with 40 or 50 meters between us. I figure maybe a little more today. Not enough, I push off and in an instant she passes me. She pulls over to wait for her crew and I pass by her gaining speed. I'm running a compact with 50 teeth on the big ring with an 11 tooth rear cog. I could use more. I'm spinning at a high cadence with little effort and I'm flying. With a following wind, not only do you travel fast, but you're exhilarated by the speed. It is a reinforcing feeling to be able to ride in your biggest gears with moderate resistance. I was back in a cocoon.

Our speed was a counterpoint to the unchanging background of mesquite and prairie grass as far as the eye can see. The Rockies and their lesser ranges are fading behind us and as long as we can keep this up, we can eat back into our deficit to the race record. We added to the distance between pulls to take advantage of our speed as we gobbled up the countryside.

Maintaining a fast tempo required concentration. Diversionary thoughts and day dreaming that occurred during tougher segments ridden at slower speeds weren't prevalent in the zone I was now in. I was focused on the road in front of me. At one point, Jim came up alongside in his photo van, stuck out his camera, began filming and tried to start an interview by asking how I was doing. I couldn't deal with the distraction. I yelled for him to get away. He got the drift and pulled ahead and I lost my chance at being on the highlight reel.

We passed through Walsh, CO after 2 hours and 40 minutes, clocking in at 25.64 mph. This was 2.3 mph faster than RMC. It would be our fastest speed between Time Stations for the whole race and to put it in perspective, Team ViaSat who passed through Walsh, 16 hours ahead of us on their record setting pace, only managed 24.08 mph. We had now shaved our deficit to RMC down to 3:01 hours. If winds remained favorable in Kansas, we could whittle that down some more.

It was while we were on this leg that those who were in the RV held the first of two meetings to discuss the current race plan and whether any changes needed to be made. Whether my comments about the uneven work load and the amount of climbing we were doing was what initiated it, I do not know. It may also have been a response to Julie and Ann's reaction to coping with a short recovery period after their Flagstaff – Tonalea segment.

Mike was there and attempted to point out my seniority in age and that I should receive some accommodation to reflect that. But, he did not have any influence on matters. Ann, in fact, pointed out that given that this was his first exposure to an endurance event, his point of view was not as informed as others. After he told me what had transpired, I was concerned. First that such a meeting would occur with no notice to me or request for input. Second, that Mike wasn't allowed to speak on my behalf and finally at Mike for pleading my case in such a way. My age was not a factor. It hadn't limited me so far and I didn't want others to think I would use it as an excuse not to contribute my share of the riding.

The nature of team rotation during RAAM meant that half the riders and crew were always on the road. Conducting any meeting on race strategy would necessarily eliminate participation of those currently riding. Joe, as Crew Chief and Julie who had taken on the role of team leader were pivotal to any changes to be made. So, the second meeting, again, involved no input from me.

Ann made the point that changing the ride schedule shouldn't sacrifice recovery time off the bike. But, if recovery was critical, it was critical for both sets of riders and Dina and I had dealt with our share of short recovery times. Further, if we truly were seeking to break the record, the race planners should have been more proactive in rider utilization. We should have focused on matching the strength of the riders to the demands of the terrain. Dina was strong, but surely, Ann was our best climber, and except for Hesperus and Yarnell, she had yet to have been extensively utilized in that role.

In the end, whatever objective the meetings had, there was no change in the predetermined schedule. So it was a non-event as far as I was concerned. I resolved to get on the bike and ride. And that is what I did.

Throwing a group of 18 people together in a close environment during a non-stop race such as RAAM will create tension and stress. Emotions are always right on the surface. There would be high highs and low lows. I tried to concentrate on the positive. I felt I was contributing a good effort to the race and increasingly accepted the schedule as pre-determined. But, I wasn't a stoic. I did want to make sure my point of view was heard. This included bringing up the race plan to those in my support crews. This now included Bill Putnam. He had replaced Paul in my vehicle as apparently, Bill preferred working with Richie as opposed to John, Dina's brother and Paul was one of Ann's buddies, so a switch was made.

During our hundred mile jaunt to Johnson City, I took the opportunity to bring to Bill's attention the uneven schedule with which we had been saddled. This had been the first time I had spoken to him directly about it and as he was designated as Co-Crew Chief, I felt I was entitled. So I pointed out the imbalance.

Bill initially had no response.

Finally, he looked back at me in the rear view mirror as I sat in the Audi between pulls.

"Amy", he said, "you've got a bad attitude. Don't ruin my RAAM".

Perish the thought.

When we had held crew and rider meetings before the race, there was a fair amount of verbalizing about the primacy of the rider's needs as far as crew responsibilities. Julie in fact joked frequently that the crew would be "her bitches". Then she would break into her laugh and everyone would giggle and laugh in turn. But during the race, things got compartmentalized as people settled into their roles. Drivers and navigators concerned themselves with following the route, which on certain days involved numerous turns as we picked our way on secondary roads through small town America. After assuring themselves that I was okay after a pull, my crew would converse amongst themselves the rest of the way and gabbed over the radio with the support crew in the other follow vehicle. While the other women on the team had advocates in their vehicles, only Richie and Paul, when he was part of my crew, seemed to have an honest concern. Now, I had Bill.

As for the rest of the crew, when not working over the bikes, Tyson concentrated on navigating the RV on its many routes that were separate from the race route and from Ft. Garland to somewhere in Kansas kept up a constant barrage of phone calls trying to figure out the best way to source a replacement crank for Julie's main bike. Jack was possessive of his role in driving the RV to the point of exhaustion and was always on the lookout for places to dump our waste water and locate sources of drinking water, ice, bread and chicken salad. And once the preplanned vehicle meeting points were imprinted in people's minds, it seemed to be one piece of the race that didn't require further decision. God forbid I would ruin someone's trip to Annapolis by expressing an opinion on something that had a critical impact on my wellbeing.

Subsequent to these "team meetings", I had one of my own with Joe. I pointed to what I believed to be an unfortunate atmosphere developing. I told him it had to stop and as Crew Chief, he was responsible for making sure it did. My conversation seemed to produce results. Interactions amongst the crew members seemed to improve. To her credit, Michelle had pointed out the support relationship I had with Mike, and he was asked to spend more time as part of my crew and either severed as navigator or rode in the back with me for the last half of the race.

We reached Johnson City a little after 1 pm Central Time. It had taken us just 4:10 hours to ride our 100.2 miles. Our speed had tailed off a little coming into the changeover point but we held close to 24 mph for the whole distance. However, the winds were becoming less favorable

We were now 16 miles inside Kansas. Dina would ride the last pull of our segment into Johnson City. I arrived in the Audi ahead of her. Mike was there to take my bike off and next to him was Julie, who would take my place. By this time, I had digested the Facebook post that proclaimed the Arizona rescue of Dina and I, by the implied sacrifice of riding most of the night. From a team perspective, this wasn't a productive post and I told her as much. Julie's crinkly smile disappeared and she appeared to cry, while trying to explain it away.

During the filming of the NBC Nightly News piece, she proclaimed that everyone on the team "loved" one another. Whether or not she believed what she said, this was the image she wanted to portray. And rightly or wrongly, if her actions or decisions were criticized, this disrupted that image and she would be wounded by that. So I reached a conclusion then that it made no sense to be critical. For the rest of the race, it would be far better to concentrate on creating the best environment for myself that I could.

Ann now took over and pulled out on the highway from a convenience store lot on the far end of a town with a skyline punctuated by grain elevators and silos. Like Dina, she had brought a time trial bike as her second bicycle and pulled it out to take advantage of the flat terrain. Initially, this seemed to work but our combined speed between Walsh and Ulysses dropped to an average of 20.8 mph. We lost a little time back to RMC.

Ulysses, KS - 3 days 11 minutes – 1,325.09 miles

It was here that the weather gods proved fickle. Zephyrus, the God of the West Wind, deserted us. He had been our benefactor in helping us hit speeds of over 25 mph. But as the high pressure ridge that produced the atmospheric conditions generating the west wind passed over us, it began to pull winds up from the Gulf and now the prevailing direction was out of the south east. Not only that, but it gathered strength and began producing gusts. Mike's check of NOAA's website for the weather ahead showed expected gusts of up to 50 mph. This was going to be trouble. We were still on the flat, flat Kansas plains; the course had an elevation change that continued to be gradually downhill in our favor and should have helped us in maintaining speed, but the winds pushed against us; holding us back.

The sudden onset of a gusting, quartering head wind was a game changer. We would now need to spend part of our energy leaning sideways into the wind, with arm and shoulder muscles tense as we grappled with the handlebar in reaction to sudden gusts. Those of us with regular bars stayed in the drops or on the hoods for better control. Ann's choice of a TT bike put her in a more aero position in the belief that this was still a time to go for speed. But her choice would prove to be ill conceived.

Our route went through wheat country and every 20 miles or so, there would be collection of grain elevators. Train tracks paralleled the highway on the north side, between these locations and in a few towns a rail spur would cross the road at an angle to reach elevators that had been placed on the other side. I wondered why that was necessary. It's not like there wasn't enough open space. But this is what we would face.

A time trial bike is set up to tilt the rider more forward and combined with her hands and elbows tucked in, there is less stability and lateral control of the bike. Ann was down on her aero bars as she came into the town of Hickok 6 miles out of Ulysses.

Page 89 of The RAAM Route Guide had the following entry:

- *6.6 Hickok "Caution Wind Currents". Grain elevators to the left.*
- *6.7 3(RR) Grain elevators to the right.*

The notorious nature of the wind currents here had made it into the Race Route Book!

Ann was down in an aero position as she streaked into town. Winds buffeted her from the side of the road where the second set of grain elevators stood. As she approached, she had to negotiate not one but 3 sets of tracks, that came from across the road at a sharp 30° angle. She crossed the first set of steel rails at the same time as she hit a wind shear caused by the elevators and went down hard.

We were in the RV on the way to the next meeting point in Ensign when a voice crackled over our radio system.

"Ann is down! She crashed."

This caught everyone's attention.

How bad were Ann's injuries? We all held our collective breath. Our plan was that if we lost a rider, we would still keep going, but this was not a pleasant thought.

Jim Harper had been filming in her follow vehicle and caught the action. Paul quickly stopped, opened the door and ran up to where Ann lay in the road. Nothing appeared broken and she was helped up and back into the Toyota. Her head had hit the pavement pretty hard and she was a little stunned at first.

Her first thoughts on falling had been that a car might hit her. Fortunately, the Toyota shielded her from that prospect. But she did rip up her shorts and pick up some road rash on her leg and knee. She remained in the van and rested while collecting herself. Gradually, she began to recover her composure and moved to the conclusion that she was going to be all right and could continue racing. After cleaning herself up and attending to her scrapes, she was ready to go.

Sometimes in these situations, the other relay partner is brought back to the point where the first rider stopped and picks up from there so as not to lose time. That was not considered in this situation. Instead, there was a timeout to assess Ann's condition. One of the decisions made was to shelve the TT bike and go back to her road frame and after the bike swap was accomplished, she climbed back on and pushed off back into the wind for the remaining distance to where Julie was waiting.

They had another 43 miles to the next Time Station in Montezuma and with the delay saw their speed drop to 16 mph. And by the time they reached Ensign, it would be 6:14 pm, still hot in the 90's and the howl of the wind was now at full song.

Dina was up first. She had followed Ann's move and had gone back to her road bike, but had also removed the aero bars. From there on out, she rode for the most part rode with her hands on the hoods and sometimes in the drops. Ann also liked to ride with her hands on the drops despite having aero bars. I had been told by Kathy early on to put aero bars on my bike and get used to them. So by the time RAAM rolled around, I had a year under my belt, so that it felt natural and comfortable and I rode pretty consistently in an aero position during the race.

There was never a discussion of riding position and wind resistance amongst the team, but the use of aero bars has been shown to increase speed by 4% or reduce energy expended by as much as 12% over normal drop bars. For riders that ride on the hoods, this discrepancy is even greater. Our team would end up averaging 42 hours per rider and a 4% improvement represents a 1 hour 40 minutes time differential. It's possible that the type of riding we were doing may not have lent itself to that much of a saving, also rider comfort is a benefit to efficiency and hence speed, but it was surprising that there wasn't a greater focus on staying in an aero position.

From Ensign, Route 56 headed Northeast toward the site of Bat Masterson's first job as a lawman, Dodge City, but we turned right and took a narrow back road due east toward Ford. The grassy shoulder was just wide enough to allow vehicles to pull off before a runoff ditch separated it from the wheat fields that ran for miles in all directions. It seemed the only thing that kept the other rider out of sight was small variations in elevation; otherwise, we could see one another from miles in the distance. I took over and began my adventure in the wind.

Just the wind noise through my helmet kept me tense. Near farmhouses and streambeds, there would be clusters of trees and shrubs and the battering and thrashing of the leaves sounded threatening. The thought of a branch, some roof shingles or other debris being blown loose and heading in my direction wasn't a comfortable thought. Holding the bike upright by leaning into the wind and trying to absorb gusts became grueling. Each time a gust hit it would move the bike sideways. No matter how many times it occurred, it gave me start each time. But I recovered, kept pedaling and waited for the next.

Fortunately, every 15 or 20 minutes, I could retreat into the sanctuary of the Audi and with the windows rolled up escape the noise, drink some liquids, eat some food and regenerate for the next pull. That put me back out in the wind on the bike 12 times that night.

I concentrated on maintaining a tempo and watching ahead in the headlights for hazards, and as I rode, I thought about the country we were passing through. I tried to imagine how tough life must have been for the women who moved west into Kansas Territory with their families a century ago. The flat unvaried prairie that they looked at every day, the cramped sod houses they lived in, the limited contact with others, the occasional Indian raid and the hard work and hardscrabble existence they must have led. And the damn wind they had to put up with.

I also recalled the stories that my father, Chuck, had told about growing up in Kansas and of the wind and dust storms of the Great Depression. I remember listening mesmerized as he told about the bad winds of '34 that blew dust all the way to New York City and the following year, the day they called Black Sunday when he said he couldn't see his hand in front of his face. Damn Wind!

In Dex Tooke's book, Unfinished Business, that covers his solo RAAM experience, he was always cussing the traffic. He hated the traffic on busy highways. He also didn't much care for the down hills either. He didn't complain about the wind. I can only assume it wasn't windy when he rode because of all the annoyances I encountered nothing was worse than the wind in Kansas.

For the next 6:01 hours we covered only 86.5 miles. It would be LS&G's longest leg time-wise. The whole ride was downhill. We would lose 900 feet of elevation. Dina and I had done two tough climbs in hot weather going into Flagstaff and covered a greater distance in less time, but pushing into the wind we couldn't get a decent rhythm or generate any speed. RMC had averaged 23 mph during this section. We could only muster 14.5 mph, which when looked at on paper seemed puny in comparison. But had we been measuring wattage, I think we generated enough to light up a small village.

After Ford, we picked up US 40 going in a southeasterly direction for 6 miles smack straight into the wind, then turned due east again. There was a good wide paved shoulder road, and we passed through several small towns which accompanied the wind with the sound of banging metal signs. We ended up in Pratt a little after mid-night. We were now in a part of the state where we could see buildings other than a grain silos that were over one story high.

Pratt – 3 days 10 hours 4 minutes – 1471.6 miles

Chapter 16

Chuck's Home Town

Ann and Julie would be riding now and would have to battle the winds for another 5 hours through the middle of the night from Pratt to Maize: another 77 miles. They would continue pushing into the wind, although at a slightly improved 16 mph. After 23 miles they crossed the Minnescah River near Calista and reached RAAM's half-way point between Oceanside and Annapolis. No celebration, just hard riding.

From Ulysses, it would take the four of us 15 hours to ride 225 miles to Maize, fighting down the highway, bucking into the wind, while grappling with the handlebars, and during that time we would lose another 5 hours to Raw Milk Cat's record.

We were nearing Wichita, so there would be a little more traffic and built up areas to negotiate.

Mike popped his head into the RV's back bedroom.

"They're 10 miles out. Let's go", he said.

I was already awake. The internal clock that we all were developing seemed to accept the intermittent limited sleep schedule we were now on. Plus you could sense a change in activity. The RV would bounce along for an hour and a half – sometimes longer - and stop. After sliding out the sides some shuffling around and settling in, there was a quiet period when everyone would sleep. But at some point, a voice could be heard on the radio as the support vehicles came into range. They would be alerting those of us in the RV that they were near. Doors would open, bikes were taken off racks, noise would come from the galley kitchen as food was prepared, muffled voices, more radio noise and by this time, I would be dressing for my upcoming ride.

By now, Dina had deserted me in the bedroom and had chosen to sleep in a bunk. Less bounce. The bunks were part of the RV that slid in and out and when it was moving, you were stuck in it even if you had to pee. Too claustrophobic for me and others, but Dina could handle it. Although on one occasion, the bunk side slide-out didn't. Dina would post in Facebook

"...resting in the coffin, but it has become sweltering hot. For some reason we can't get me out....."

I guess we eventually did.

As I pulled on my jersey, I could feel stiffness in my shoulders, upper arms and neck from fighting the wind. What limited massage time I had received from Michelle helped some, but it wasn't enough. Solo riders can develop what is called "Shermer's Neck", which is an acute weakness of the neck muscles that makes it difficult to hold one's head up without physical support. One solution that women have used is to braid a pony tail and tie it to their bra strap to support the neck. Relay riders haven't experienced the problem. Thank heavens for that, I have short hair.

Mike had toasted a bagel for me and slathered on peanut butter and jelly. Even though it was still early it was already warm.

"Wind's changing", Mike was looking at the NOAA weather app on his iPhone.

"The forecast for Wichita, calls for winds out of the south west at 10 to 15", he continued.

"Piece of cake", he said with a smile and looked at me.

That was good news. The wind had swung around in our favor and would now be a quartering tailwind.

In no time we were out on the road waiting for the exchange in front of a Qwik Stop in the little town of Maize. Ann arrived first in the Toyota and switched out with Dina. Joe and Susan took the Toyota in to top off the gas tank. A few minutes later, I could see head lights coming slowly down the road. Mike was holding my bike and stepped back as I grabbed it. I threw a leg over, clipped in my right food and looked back. It was 5 am, so we were required to do a standing exchange.

Once again, my stomach experienced the flip flops of pre-race anxiety. The wind had shifted, but what other adversities would I run into this time out. Julie came up, stopped and I pushed off, gathering speed and dropped into my aero bars.

"Go Amy", I heard in the distance from behind me.

I did, and once more, after I settled into a rhythm, I knew it was going to be a good ride.

As Mike had predicted, the wind had turned favorable. We were on our way to Eureka in the Flint Hills of Eastern Kansas an easy 67 miles. Not much grew in the thin limestone soils of the area and open land with few trees stretch to the north and the south. We would by-pass Wichita on the north and ride through the little towns of Kechi, Benton and Towanda. It was a good road, divided and a big shoulder on the right. I was on the bike when we came toward Interstate 35 and passed under it.

The music coming out of the loudspeaker stopped. Richie's voice came on.

"Amy, you're gonna' want to turn left after the "landfill" sign, at the light", he said.

I looked up and saw the intersection he was talking about and waved. The music came back on. It was a Leonard Cohen song. Leonard is one of my favorites. It was on Bill's play list, which helped to improve his standing. Then a green sign with the town name "El Dorado - Pop. 13,021" came into view. I knew we were going to go through El Dorado. It was where Chuck grew up. But when I saw the sign, a wave of emotion hit me. I got a lump in my throat and my eyes got teary as I thought about him.

His father had moved the family here from Oklahoma to work in the oil field that was discovered in 1915, which, by the time the U.S. entered World War I, had become the world's largest producer. It's where he got the idea to become an oil wildcatter.

I had entertained myself with his dust bowl stories on the way through Kansas, but seeing the El Dorado sign, brought his memory back like a brick. I remember him reminiscing about his dog, Hambone, who used to jump out of his Model T and chase after all manner of distractions, which required Chuck to stop the car and run after him to resolve whatever situation he had gotten into. He had a gift as a story teller and could make a boring day sound like the most exciting time there ever was. It felt good to reach back to these memories. He died of cancer 20 years ago, but I could feel his spirit that day. He had brought the good wind and gave me positive energy and I put it to use.

Each time on the bike that morning I channeled that good energy into my cycling and Dina and I exceeded 23 mph during the stretch from Maize to El Dorado and finished the 67 mile ride to Eureka in just over 3 hours. The Kansas prairie winds ended any chance that we would break the record set by RMC, but it was nice to see that we pulled almost an hour back on them during that ride.

I closed out the leg riding into Eureka and handing off to Julie just after 8 am. They would have a 5 hour 91 mile turn to Fort Scott through rolling croplands.

Fort Scott was an early outpost on the eastern edge of Kansas; it represented the first stop in the new Territory and provided protection to early settlers on the way in. It would be our last stop on the way out. We were happy to leave the wind behind and as Dorothy said to Toto "....we're not in Kansas anymore". I said to myself, "Thank God."

Mike had been sending text messages to a few of a number of people who were generous in their support. One was an old friend, Tom Murphy.

Tom responded and asked how I was holding up.

"Amy is incredible." Mike texted back, "After this morning's ride, first time she said she was tired. Cross winds gave us problems yesterday, lost time. Incredible, incredible."

I would now have five hours of recovery time, which I could use.

Before I crawled into bed, there was a small crisis. Ann's follow vehicle got a big nail stuck in its tire on the way into Fort Scott. It was changed quickly, no easy task as the Toyota van's spare is under the floor in the middle of the vehicle. It was one of those mini wheels, which was not going to hold up for very long. On hearing of this problem, Tyson ran down some tire repair equipment in town to include a plug and some tire goo. No sooner had the Toyota pulled in than 4 of our crew rushed to it, jacked it up, took off the spare as Tyson plugged the hole and re-inflated the tire in no time at all. So far, we were having good fortune in solving our vehicle problems.

Chapter 17

Show Me

Dina started our next leg in Fort Scott at 1 pm and we would ride to Hermitage, MO a distance of 82 miles in 4 ½ hours. We now left the one dimensional flat straight roads of Kansas for a more varied topography. The route had lots of rollers, short climbs and descents of 50 to 100 feet and lots of turns. We would also be passing through many small towns along Highway 54.

One of those towns was Nevada, a town burned down by Union militia during the Civil War border conflicts that also hit Fort Scott. It saw the coming of the railroad with both the Missouri Pacific and the Missouri Kansas and Texas (Katy) connecting there in the 1870s, about the same time the State Mental Asylum was opened.

We also we hit the 4 day mark. As we began to reel through major mileage or time metrics, the closer the finish line would seem. It fueled a rising anticipation. Success was coming closer to our grasp. No longer did I see myself as a small dot on the road with a huge expanse in front of me. The finish was within reach now.

Before I left, I had checked my Facebook page that Mike had been updating. My company had sales meetings on Wednesday mornings and I got a number of supportive comments that day. People were getting caught up in the excitement of my adventure and of the team's progress. This added to the positive energy I picked up in El Dorado. These posts were a real morale booster. It was about at this time that Mike's daughter Kirsten wrote her exhortation, "Ride, Amy, Ride!" It became Mike's cheer as I whizzed by. I got messages and tweets, I was trending! Steven Colbert was now following me on Twitter.

It was hot and humid, but manageable. The variety of the country we were going through now, replaced the monotony of the last 500 miles. As I took each pull, I needed to be more conscious of what was happening around me. The tailwind we had enjoyed in eastern Kansas, however, turned against us yet again as we had picked up a quartering head wind. But compared with our experience in the preceding state it wasn't bad. Our speed began to settle in in the 18 to 19 mph range.

We were nearing the Ozark Mountains and crossed several rivers and lakes. The road kill changed from the occasional rabbit to frogs and armadillos. There were lots of dead armadillos. Later that evening, Dina thought that what she was seeing were alligators before she was assured they were not.

During this leg, Jack found an accommodating RV park that allowed us to dump out the black water, which had been sloshing around near the almost filled mark for the better part of the day. It limited on board bathroom use to riders only. Mike had heated up brisket, which he served with some noodles and a salad to those of the crew with the RV. He was still making an effort to not only to keep my food container filled with what I nibbled on during my shift, but those of the support crews. It was a little problematic to manage this process as some of the crew took care of making sandwiches for themselves, while others grabbed the sandwiches Mike had made and left in the refrigerator.

The riders and crew had a variety of meal choices. Michelle had prepared a great deal of it and frozen it before the trip. There were burritos with sausage and meatless burritos, there were broiled chicken breasts. There were; big bags of Spanish rice, meatballs and big jars of spaghetti sauce and of course spaghetti, which was stored in an overhead area behind some clothing bags that wasn't found until we were somewhere in Ohio. There were vegetarian bean patties for the riders that I don't think anyone ate. There were several casserole dishes that had been frozen. The brisket was provided by one of my co-workers, Dagley Arnold. In addition there was a variety of sandwich makings; sliced ham, roast beef, turkey and a choice of cheeses for sandwiches. And bread, loaves of bread and bagels, pretzels, chips and trail mix.

On top of which, with the concern that we would run out of food, which turned out not to be a risk in the slightest, the volunteer run from Denver to Weston in the middle of the night to deliver food, brought more than we could store and half of it went back. Once we began to go through areas of higher population density, we found resupply to not be a problem.

Despite this cornucopia, there were complaints about how many sandwiches got made before each turnover, the sandwich meat selection, the amount of mayonnaise and the like. Moreover, a contingent preferred Wal-Mart chunky chicken salad with grapes sandwiches, which in turn rendered the stores of other sandwich meat unnecessary. I tried the coveted chicken salad sandwich and concluded it was an acquired taste, which I hadn't.

The decision to have choices stands in stark contrast to the Fuzzy Mitchell turkey sandwich solution, which made for less complexity and minimized complaints. In our situation, the onboard refrigerator freezer was stuffed to overflowing as were two iced coolers in the outside compartments. Anytime a decision was made to serve one or another item, a hunt through these various spaces to find the item in question was begun. It was hard to discern what was in the wrapper or container requiring repeated searches for the called for food item. And once found and prepared, it was not always what was desired. Fuzzy would be appalled

At 5:30 pm, we pulled into a gravel lot by Casey's General Store in Hermitage handing off to Team B. They would be on for 91 miles to Jefferson City. The route swung in a northeast direction with rollers having a 200-300 foot elevation change as they worked their way across the streams and rivers that fed the Lake of the Ozarks and several arms of the Lake itself. They would finish the ride in just under 5 hours averaging 18.8 mph.

Jefferson City – 1880.6 miles - 4:08:13

When we reached Jefferson City, despite the late hour, the Time Station was lit up by a TV crew recording the arrival of racers. It was at a gas station and local enthusiasts had lined the curb with paper bag and candle lit luminarias making it quite festive.

It was also here that a clutch of RAAM racers would come through at nearly the same time. Up until now, we had jockeyed positions with some of the relay teams that started with us. The four man Equipe Schwarz guys were still just ahead of us with a British team, The 4 Beefeaters just behind them. Several 8 person teams were also near us, Stormwind, a mixed team with 4 adults and 4 teenagers, Wounded Warrior Project one of the teams that had us choke back some emotion when they were introduced in Oceanside, and Above + Beyond Cancer, that included 6 men and 2 women under 50.

However, when we reached the center of Missouri, we began to pass the slower solo riders that had left Oceanside several days before we did. This made for some excitement as other crews cheered us from the side of the road and we cheered them. If you saw a member of another team ahead of you on the road who might be catchable, you might start to mash the pedals just a little bit harder. Crossing paths with another competitor offered a brief moment of camaraderie before returning to the isolation of grinding away down the road by oneself. Looks were brief and words rarely exchanged, but empathy and support were palpable.

That night, as we waited for Julie to come in, two solo riders came through. First, an Italian, Valario Zamboni followed 3 minutes later by Gunnar Ohlanders, the Ultra-Cycling Viking from Sweden. Their crews sprang into action, taking their bikes for a check, leading them into a waiting RV for a quick rest and nourishment, then both were back on the bike and off. They had spent only a couple minutes off the bike to regroup. There was a crowd of several hundred people that had gathered to witness the scene and greeted each arrival with a welcoming cheer. Racers spend a great deal of time alone in the saddle, but when you come across this level of attention it created special moments that stuck in your mind.

Several minutes after Gunnar took off; we saw the telltale ultra-white LED headlights of the Audi with the pinpoint light of Julie's bike light 10 meters in front. She turned the corner and went up a small hill where Dina sat waiting. Then Dina was off. She was riding her time trial bike.

The Audi went to the station to top off the gas. Mike rolled my bike up and put it on the rear rack and I was about to climb into the back when a rider from the Above + Beyond Cancer team rolled in. This is an advocacy group, much like Lance Armstrong's LiveStrong charity. But unlike the latter entity, they organize adventures for cancer survivors to include treks in the Himalayas to places like the Everest base camp and of course this year's RAAM.

As the finishing rider came in, he rolled to a stop alongside the team mate who would be next to ride and emphatically stated,

"I'm Bob Irving and I'm a cancer survivor"!

He then reached up and high-fived his team mate's upraised hand. Then, the new rider took off and continued up the small hill to the cheers of our small crowd. It was a magic moment.

Jefferson City, the state capitol lies next to the Missouri River and is the beginning of the 'Missouri Rhineland', which runs east toward the Mississippi River. The steep hillsides and residual limestone soil are similar to its German namesake. The area was settled by Germans in the early 1800's and before Prohibition was the second largest wine producing region in the U.S behind Ohio of all places. Only recently has it begun to redevelop its vineyards.

But we wouldn't see the vines or enjoy any wine tasting as we would do a late night stretch starting at 10:30 CST finishing in the town of Washington 4 ½ hours later. More rollers as we turned off Highway 54, a divided road with wide shoulders onto Hwy 94 a 2 lane road with no shoulders, which paralleled the Missouri River bottom lands. It was flat to downhill as we closed in on the Big Muddy. The Mississippi River wasn't far now.

Small woods and croplands were on either side of us and not far away running parallel to our route was the old MKT railroad right of way that is now a 240 mile bikeway called the 'Katy Trail'.

Dina had ended up on her time trial bike for a reason. Before starting out, she had noticed uneven shifting of her rear derailleur. Tyson was told and he being the thorough mechanic that he was, tried to dial in the shifting before she left. When adjustments to tension and limit screw settings didn't do the trick, like all good wrenches, he took the derailleur off and started from scratch. He nearly got everything back together, but time ran out. Julie was getting close to our exchange point in Jeff City and with Dina up first, the tension began to rise.

Someone had fortunately pulled her TT bike off the back of the RV just in case. Finally, when the radio announced that Julie was 1 mile out, Tyson dropped everything and grabbed her TT bike, quickly checked the shifting, gave the tires a couple of pump strokes of air and ran it out to the road just in time. Julie came in ten seconds later and Dina sailed off into the night. The route circled the capitol area and the lights were blinding making the road hard to see, but with the added adrenalin of the last minute bike switch she was up to the task.

She had to negotiate about a dozen 100 to 200 foot steep rollers on our route over a rougher road than we had been on previously, that included a bunch of twists and turns. Not ideal terrain for a TT bike, but Dina shrugged and just powered through it.

Tyson had gotten her bike back together and tuned a couple minutes after she pulled out. Mike grabbed the bike and put it inside the RV for a quick change out on the road. Unfortunately, the road was so narrow that the RV was shunted to a large vehicle alternate. It was much longer than the racers route. A wrong turn by Jack, forced a requirement to back track complete with difficult turn around with minimal clearance. This doubled the 77 miles that Dina and I covered that night. So the RV and Dina's bike arrived at our destination in Washington, MO a few minutes before we did.

Our team mates took over there and would head into St. Charles County. Race organizers warned us about this area. Earlier in the year, several county commissioners had attempted to ban all cycling in the county. Stories from other cyclists had told of incidents with motorists where they attempted to run riders off the road. While we didn't have any confrontations that dangerous, Julie and Ann were not immune to shouted profanities as they rode by. Joe subsequently sent a letter to the local paper in protest and at least he did receive an apologetic response.

They reached the Mississippi River Time Station a minute before 7 am EST and crossed together over a cable suspension bridge named for William Clark of the Corps of Discovery. Lewis and Clark had started their historic expedition to the Pacific Coast from a site near the confluence of the Missouri River just 3 miles south of our route. They would sail up and return 2 years later on the same river we had paralleled on our way here. We were now only 2 days and 963 miles from the Atlantic Coast.   The next stop was Hamel, Illinois.

Chapter 18

Home Folks

The route we would be taking through southern Illinois would pass through Greenville. At one time Chuck had interests in some oil leases in the area and it lay due north on a straight line up Hwy. 127 from my hometown of Nashville, IL where my Mother still lives. Greenville was also a Time Station. Before the race had started, I had given this information to my brother Scott in the hopes they would come up and see me ride by. Had we been close to the RMC record, it would have been in the middle of the night. So until I had a better sense of when we would get there, no specific plan was formulated and I thought it was best to play it by ear. As it turned out, we were now a little over 10 hours behind RMC, so it would at least be sometime in the morning. But with my preoccupation with all that was going on, I hadn't contacted Scott or my Mother with a plan as to just when and where we might meet.

The RV had parked in the lot of the CC Food Mart and Service Station in Hamel just 20 miles past the Mississippi. As I was getting ready for my ride that morning, it struck me that I hadn't followed through on contacting them and had an instant pang of regret. Here, I was so close to home and my family. During the race, emotions are right under the surface and I now had this hollow feeling. I was annoyed with myself and embarrassed by my inattention to those that had supported the team so generously. But more than anything, I wanted to see them.

Mike said that he had given updates to Scott and told him that there would be a rider exchange in Hamel around 8:00 am. He thought Scott might try to meet up with us here. Although they might also try to catch us in Greenville about 25 miles further on. He didn't know.

Despite his confidence that Scott was going to try and catch up with us at some point, I wasn't totally convinced and it weighed on me.

Conjuring up memories of Chuck spirited me through the Flint Hills of Kansas and seeing folks from home would give me an emotional boost to start the last third of the race here in my home state. But so far, no one had appeared.

Mike had gone to get my bike off the back of the RV and was rolling it across the parking area toward the road when I came down the steps of the RV. I looked around the lot hoping to see a familiar car, but saw nothing. I followed Mike across the road to where he had positioned the bike and snapped my helmet strap. Ann would be finishing and I would be first out on the road, but she was still 4 or 5 miles out.

Just then, I saw my Mother's red SUV coming toward us. It turned into a parking area just in front of me. I could see the Illinois vanity plates, TE 77 on the back. My brother Scott had brought my Mother and her friend Audrey and Audrey's 2 daughters, Ann and Sarah, up from Nashville. What a joy to see them. I couldn't contain myself and ran to their car when they stopped with a big smile on my face. What a lift. As they all got out, one by one I gave everyone a hug and thanked them for coming. Up until now, it had been memories and Facebook posts that cheered me on, but the human touch is so much more powerful.

We began chatting excitedly and some of the crew waiting to change-over came up and I introduced everyone.

Then my Mother asked, "Well? Are you having any problems? Are you holding up all right?"

I smiled. "I'm fine, Mother. Everything is going fine."

She was the one who had deemed me too old in her annual Christmas letter. So naturally, this would be on her mind. Normally, this point of view might have annoyed me, but this morning, I loved it.

She had also brought along several boxes of home-made chocolate chip cookies, which she gave to Mike. So corny. So clichéd. So wonderful.

Soon enough, the Audi came in with Julie inside and pulled across the street to gas up. After topping off, one of the Dave's pulled the car back behind me.

Mike would be navigating for Bill this leg and had already gotten in, and as Ann pulled in and I took off, he got on the loudspeaker and thanked the Nashville crowd, hooked up his iPod and put on Arlo Guthrie's version of "The City of New Orleans" which includes the line, 'we'll be gone 500 miles when the day is done', and followed me down the highway. Not quite 500 today, but close.

After a tour of the RV, Scott and his passengers followed us down the road as we traveled toward Greenville and stopped during several of my rider transitions to prolong the visit. There were several teams around us during this section so there was a good show for them to see. We traded leads with Above + Beyond several times and we passed one of the solo riders. To have an in person view of the race must have been exciting for them as it was a morale booster for me. Although, Mike told me that after I had taken off after one exchange, Bill almost ran over my Mother when she inadvertently stepped in front of the Audi.

With all the hometown energy, we carried good speed over the next 75 miles and averaged 20 mph for the first time since El Dorado, reaching our next vehicle meeting point in Effingham, IL in 3:45 hours. Effingham, aptly enough, is a train stop on "City of New Orleans" Route. And in keeping with women's achievements, the home of Ada Kepley, who in 1870, became the first woman to graduate from law school in America. However, Illinois law denied her the right to practice. How times have changed. She wrote poetry, published her autobiography and was deeply involved in the women's suffrage movement. Unfortunately, she ended up as a temperance advocate as well, probably causing the replanting of those early Missouri vineyards. No power lunches with martinis for Ada.

We were also just north of the Cahokia Mounds, the remains of one of the grandest, most advanced Indian cities in North America. It occupied 6 square miles and in its heyday in the period 1000-1200 AD, had a Mississippian culture population that peaked at 20,000 people making it larger than any European city at the time. It contained 120 massive hand built earthen mounds, many of which still stand and a cedar post calendar circle array, equivalent to Stonehenge. The fertility of the land and cultivation of crops was a key to the cities longevity but by 1400 AD climate change and depleted resources led to the site being abandoned.

We were leaving that behind as well as we pedaled east down Hwy 40. We were now in an area where following the route was becoming critical. At one point that day, Bill missed a turn ignoring Mike's guidance and coming in to Effingham, Mike missed one as well. Each time that happened, I would have to get off the bike and be driven back to the route before continuing on. Route guidance was becoming more critical. Sections between time stations would now include a dozen or more turns. Some were obvious, others seemed counterintuitive. Fortunately our navigators were on top of the route and that was one of the few times we had an issue.

It was just before noon when Team B took over. They had 73 miles to go to reach Sullivan, Indiana. We were in farm country. Lots of soybean and corn fields along the way. The terrain was rolling, still humid and hot, but they exceeded 20 mph during their leg as they took advantage of the easier flat roads.

Sullivan, IN – 5:01:09 – 2,197.92 miles

We have now been on the bikes for 5 days with just 2 days and 800 miles to go. Dina and I took over in Sullivan at 4:20 EST for another 3 ½ hour ride to cover 68 miles. These rides were now shorter than Fuzzy's 4 hour "optimal" ride/recovery discipline. Given the flatter topography, it would have seemed that staying at 4 hours would improve efficiency, but at this stage of the race, when things, according to Bill, can easily go awry, we stayed with the "plan".

We were still passing solo riders and it was near Switz City, when I was on the bike, that I began to close in on someone's follow vehicle. I pulled around it and came up to the rider in front. It was Len Forkas, the founder of the HopeCam Charity. As I pedaled by him we exchanged looks and nods. He appeared haggard and labored more slowly on the bike. As I continued by him, I felt thankful that I was on a relay team and could enjoy time off the bike. Len would go on to finish first in the 50-59 age group that year in a time of 11 days 4 hours and 47 minutes.

There were lots of small hills on rural 2 lane roads with narrow shoulders and Richie had to pinpoint 11 turns as we pushed through small towns. Traffic was moderate but noticeable. We also went through Bloomfield before reaching our next exchange point in Bloomington. 'Bloom' seemed to be popular in town names. There must have been a lot of flowery forest plants like trillium, sweet cicely and baneberry when these areas were first settled.

It was also probably pretty green as well. We went through a number of "Greens' during the race, villes, boros, woods and we would pass through Greenburg before hitting our next vehicle meeting point in Batesville. Mike was familiar with the town because as a research analyst on Wall Street, he had followed Hil-Rom, a manufacturer of hospital beds. He pointed out to me that should things get a little sticky and go from bad to worse, it would be okay because for a small town, they had terrific patient care facilities and when all else failed, it was also home to the world's largest casket manufacturer. What a pill. Sometimes laughter, or attempts to induce a laugh, doesn't result in the best medicine.

We ended in Bloomington and handed off to Julie and Ann. They would have a 77.5 mile leg and averaged just under 18 mph. It was here that RMC slowed to 10 mph. In fact, they actually stopped because of a traffic tie-up caused by an accident that was blocking the race's progress. At the end, they had 3 hours and 23 minutes subtracted from their overall finishing time, which seemed like a lot. This was an estimate of the time they lost and it gave them added recovery time, which affirms that luck is part of the equation of success in this race.

Looking back, there were really only two regions where we lost big chunks of time to them. The first was at the start and into the Sonoran Desert where we dealt with Santa Ana conditions and they had favorable tail winds. We also followed a race plan that put a lot of the burden of riding in the desert heat on just one pair of riders. The second was when we hit the head winds in Kansas. We clawed back over an hour in our home state of Colorado, and we took back another piece in El Dorado, and several sections in Indiana, but other than that, they seemed to have been a little stronger. After Kansas until reaching Illinois we had averaged just less than 19 mph while RMC was averaging above 20. They had been smiled upon by Zephyrus, while we got stuck with Eurus, the unlucky God of the East Winds.

Our next slot was from Batesville to Lebanon, OH, a 66 mile stretch that we started a little after mid-night and reeled off in 4 hours. We were now moving from rural landscapes to more developed areas and would make some two dozen turns as we snaked our way along minor roads to avoid traffic and congestion. It didn't help the speed and we dropped below 17 mph.

Mid-way through the ride, we went through Oxford, the home of Miami University. The architecture and the tree lined townscape suggested a more gentrified environment and I found myself feeling the influence of the eastern part of the country. Four young guys, shirtless, sitting on a porch smoking cigarettes looked up distractedly as I rode past and returned to their conversation as if I was normal fare for 2 am in the morning. One of them gave a "shaka" greeting by waving his hand with thumb and pinky extended. Certain scenes that I observed crossing the country would vividly stick in my mind. I think because of, rather than in spite of being a rather ordinary incident, it became poignant.

Team B was on for the early morning 78 mile ride to Chillicothe that would take 4 ½ hours. Their speed dropped to under 16 mph. There were some hills in this section, but the climbs were short with no more than 300 feet gained on the biggest.

Chillicothe is named after the principle tribal settlement of the Shawnee Indians. It is at a location in the Scioto River valley that has been occupied by American Indians for nearly 3,000 years.

Chillicothe, OH – 2486.4 miles - 5:17:39

We woke up at to a light rain and would start our ride at 8:50 am. Up until now, I had done my best riding during this time of the day. But we were now in the home stretch. The intermittent sleeping pattern and the bouncing bed in the RV were beginning to wear on me. While the rain offered relief to the heat and humidity of the past several days it wasn't welcome. It was an irritant.

Dina had started and I was driven ahead to the first rider exchange. My stomach went through its normal routine of flip flops as I eyed the wet road ahead, waiting for her to arrive. I had a helmet cover and a rain jacket, but putting on rain gear only captured heat and retained the moisture inside. I needed to muster up a positive frame of mind to deal with the day's weather.

This section was hilly with many challenging short climbs. We had left behind flat terrain where we could shoot along at 20 mph or more. We were now in a place of rivers and streams and varying terrain.

On my second pull, I came to a construction area reducing the road to one lane. A flagman stopped me for oncoming traffic. Rain was peppering my helmet and dripped off my nose. My butt and crotch was wet from the wheels throwing up spray off the road. My mood was being test by the gloomy weather. But once the flagman waved me through, I was back in the saddle, picking up a tempo, climbing and then descending through pastures and cornfields, wooded hills and through small towns. Small streambeds bisected the road or paralleled us alongside. If it weren't for the weather, this was very pretty country. I focused on that.

We not only received data on our speed between Time Stations, but race officials also computed our cumulative average as well. Over the first several days this measure had crept up to 18.36 mph before we hit Kansas but had dropped below 18 mph as we fought through the wind. We now were rallying and reached an average of 18.15 mph at the Bloomington Time Station. Could we hold on to our speed as we began to climb toward the Appalachians, our last major obstacle?

Dina and I finished our ride on the Appalachian Highway that parallels the Hocking River in Guysville, Ohio, a small mill town on the western flanks of mountains. We arrive at 1:00 pm in the afternoon.

Chapter 19

Appalachian Hill Climbing Festival

From Guysville, Team B has a 20 mile ride to the West Virginia state line. They will be passing through a menagerie of town names: Ratcliffburg, Elk Fork and Deerwalk and near the State Park on Blennerhasset Island in the middle of the Ohio River near Parkersburg. This is where Aaron Burr and Harman Blennerhasset planned their "Conspiracy". They stored supplies and trained a company of men to lead to Louisiana Purchase territory with the objective of establishing a separate nation. Burr was an opportunistic sort, hoping to resurrect his fortunes after being dropped from the Vice Presidential slot on Jefferson's ticket and getting bad press for killing Alexander Hamilton in their famous duel. The Ohio Militia and treason charges put a stop to his plans.

Parkersburg, lies on the western side of the Appalachian Plateau. It serves as our doorway to the numerous parallel ridges caused by the trellis shaped drainage systems of its rivers and streams; topography over which we will now climb, descend and repeat.

The Route book advertises this stretch as the most difficult climbing of the race.

Not a RAAM story has been told that doesn't dwell on the difficulty here. The saving grace, if it could be called that, was that it would be the last challenging sector we would ride. Before we got to the Atlantic Coast littoral, we would have 250 miles of this kind of terrain and have to deal with a climb every 5 or 6 miles, 30 of which were tough affairs of up to 1,500 feet in elevation gain. They would include the steepest grades we have yet to face.

By the time Team B finished their 66.7 mile ride to West Union, they will have experienced more elevation change than on any other Time Station segment of the race including the Rockies. All of which was between 587 and 1,205 feet above sea level. Yet because of the down hills, they averaged almost 19 mph for the segment ending in West Union. They had passed the TS at Ellensboro, WV at 4:02 pm in the afternoon.

Ellenboro, WV - 2612.28 miles – 6 days 00:51 hours

We're now into the sixth day and we only have 381 miles to go. If we can average 16 mph, we can break the 7 day barrier. That shouldn't be difficult. We're averaging 2 mph over that. It would seem to be an achievable objective, but we have the Appalachians to get over.

And we are dealing with fatigue. Ride/Recovery intervals have varied, but have recently been around the 4 hour optimum. However, the extended deep sleep that my body now craves remains limited.

The rider exchange in West Union is at the bottom of descent that follows a sharp 300 foot climb. Julie finished the ride and Dina and I took over at 5 pm. We started on a divided 4 lane highway, US 50, with a wide shoulder. After 20 miles we turned off the to follow a narrow 2 lane road that requires 10 turns in 8 miles. More secondary roads through rural landscapes leads us to Grafton, which marks Time station 46. Although it was getting dark, the town's historic, well-preserved 1800's architecture appeared as if from another era.

The first settler here arrived in the late 1700's. He was an Irish immigrant named James Current who traded a horse for 1,300 acres and had a young lad survey it for him. A fellow named George Washington. The section of US 50 we're now traveling on a highway named for our first President.

But our speed at just over 15 mph, lagged our objective.

We finish our 69 mile segment traversing knobs and hollows that ended with a 1,300 foot 6% climb up Thornton's Hill and cresting Friend's Gap before a 9% descent to Cool Springs back in West Virginia. At least we weren't dealing with the heat of the day. It took us 4 hours 40 minutes to finish the ride which ended at 9:40 pm.

Climbing into the RV, I had a hot plate of spaghetti and meatballs, before crawling into the bed in back. Michelle was running out of energy. The short massages she had been administering after our rides were no longer offered. Others are feeling it as well. Mike took over for Jack in navigating the RV after he fell asleep at his post. At one point during the night with Julie on the bike, the headlights of the Audi behind her began to drift into the oncoming lane. Richie had to grab the wheel to straighten the car out. Bill had fallen asleep.

In one of the scenes from Jim Harper's video, Bill responded to a question about problems the crew might encounter supporting riders.

"Well, I suppose running them over would be bad," was his reply.

Yes it would have.

Speaking of Jim, he had fired John as his driver. Despite pulling off most nights and getting sleep at a motel before catching back up, Jim's impatience with John's driving style got the best of him.

So he took over. Despite all this fraying at the edges, we continued to close in on Annapolis.

Our speed over the next 67 miles wouldn't improve. Ann and Julie rode through a large expanse of state forests on US 50 with several hard climbs to keep them busy. When they passed through Keyser, our combined average from Grafton was only 14.7 mph. Our next meeting point was in Cresaptown, MD.

As I got ready to ride at 2 in the morning on that last day, I could feel the miles in my legs. I pulled on my shorts, zipped up my jersey and wiggled my feet into my bike shoes. It took a little more effort than the last time. When I sat down at the banquette in the kitchen area I stared at the bagel in front of me. A cup of hot tea helped. Caffeine gives me the jitters so I'm not a coffee person. I stayed with this approach although I probably could have benefited from a jolt right then.

Mike had my bike out. Ann was on her way in. I'm out first. We're in the parking area of a Sheetz Convenience Store and I made my way out to the road where we will change out riders. The neon glow of the 24 hour store, radiated on several aging clapboard houses across the road. The town, which sprawls along the highway in both directions, is named after Colonel Cresap, the colorful "Rattlesnake Colonel", who fought against the French, the Catabwa Indians and European settlers from Pennsylvania in equal measure. Despite his eagerness to fight battles, he was also known as "Big Spoon" by the Indians because of his generosity.

This is the second time we've been in Maryland as we've crisscrossed the border with West Virginia and the Potomac River several times now. But we're out of West Virginia for good.

As Ann approached, my normal bout of apprehension hit, but as I pushed off and began pedaling, I sought to get back in a groove. The fear that I would get to a point at which physical and mental exhaustion would make me unable to get back on the bike, that I would lie down on the side of the road somewhere and refuse to go on, hadn't completely gone away. The elephant was still there.

But I kept climbing back on and after a few minutes of pedaling, I'd begin to realize that the legs were still good, and that I was okay for another go.

But tonight, the legs didn't feel as strong and thinking of the climbing we've done and what was ahead, I worried.

After a quarter mile, the road began to steepen. Not much of a warm up. I ground up the hill for 2 miles in a low gear and handed off to Dina. She will have another mile or so to the top. Dave Ells took my bike and I got in the back and slumped in my seat and closed my eyes to rest. Dina took the 5 mile downhill to the outskirts of Cumberland and on into the center of town. We have been heading northeast and now swing east on the old U.S. 40, the National Highway. Cumberland was a jumping off point for westward migration 150 years ago as it was one of the major gateways through the Allegheny Escarpment that provided a route for early Americans migrating into the Ohio River Valley.

Logically, it should be an exit from the difficult terrain we've now passed through, but it is not. Cumberland marks Time Station 48. This is the beginning of a 37.1 mile segment ending in Hancock, long considered the toughest of all the Appalachian sections of RAAM. The late Jure Robic, a five time winner, often said that he looked forward to this part of the race course, because he could use his reserves of power to pull away from anyone still close to him. To recognize his memory, Race organizers began awarding a trophy in his name to the individual with the fastest time and this would be the second year it would be given.

The section consists of four major climbs with steep following down hills that take away all the hard earned altitude, without allowing for much recovery before the next hill looms. "Cruel" is the adjective often used by solo racers. I have several miles of modest climbing coming out of town before it starts getting steep and we trade-off several times climbing the 1,000 feet of Rocky Gap. Several miles further on, another 600 feet at an 8% grade greets us going up Polish Mountain, followed by another 900 feet of an 8 per-center with a false summit called, rather benignly, Town Hill 1680.

We're doing 1 to 2 mile pieces on the climbs, but whoever is on for the downhill goes all the way to the bottom. I could really feel the exertion needed on Town Hill and my legs began to hurt. My lungs were trying to suck oxygen out of the thick air. My mind was telling me to stop this nonsense. After my pull, I got back in the Audi and we drove up the road for the next one. I didn't know how many hills we had to do that night. I just got out of the car, threw my leg over the top tube and began to grind away as best I could. But the next hill, I was told, was the last.

We crossed a creek and start heading up a steep grade before pulling over to the side. I waited for what seems a long time before I saw Dina's silhouette in the Toyota's headlights as she clawed her way upward on the beginning of Sideling Hill.

"It's hard," she said as she stopped alongside me.

The Route Book says, that this hill 'could be a walker'.

I stood on the pedals to get the bike moving. The quietness of the night was broken by the loud speakers that serenaded me with a playlist I have heard over and over for the last week. I shut the sound out. Conversation between me and the crew was limited to occasional words of encouragement when I start out. Tonight they say nothing. And with no turns, there is no need for guidance over the loudspeaker. I am left to finish the last section of Sideling Hill in semi-isolation.

As I pedaled upwards, I began to feel strange. Sleep deprivation and a depletion of energy reserves will have an effect. Hallucinations, delusions and schizophrenia do occur during this race. One year, late at night while riding near this very place, the great Robic himself experienced a bout of paranoia, threw his bike into the bushes and yelled at his crew to get away from him. He thought they were conspiring against him. Dina had visual hallucinations. She thought that the dead armadillos were alligators chasing her down the road when we came through Missouri.

In my case, I experienced tactile hallucinations. My feet and my hands felt like they were leaving my body and moving away from me. My lips became numb. The road went unrelentingly straight up on the west side of the mountain, but it didn't look like it was going up. I felt vertiginous. Outside my headlight cone, twilight lightened the skies above the dark shadows of the trees. Doubts formed in my mind. But then, up above, in the distance, I saw light against the trees. It gave me perspective. The light came from car headlights that weren't moving. It's just around a long sweeping turn at the top. I knew it was the Toyota and Dina waiting for me.

The steepness of the road was sucking out what is left of my energy. I was jittery and light headed and kept fighting the urge to stop and end the pain. I continued pushing the pedals as I climbed up the hill.

The Toyota was a magnet. The blinking yellow lights on the top of it finally came into view. If I could see it, I could make it. A quarter of a mile now............two hundred yards............one hundred.......I saw Dina, standing in the headlights. I drew up alongside of her, unclipped my left foot as I rolled to a stop, and put it down heavily on the road and then my right   She started riding toward the upcoming descent and the Toyota dutifully fell in behind her.

My head dropped and a flood of relief filled my body. I rested my forehead on the back of my hands still clutching the top of the handlebar. I was taking in big gulps of air. I stood there not moving. It wasn't a choice, I was spent.

Gradually, I began to move and lifted my leg over the bike. Someone took it and I walked back toward the Audi. I climbed in, slumped down and reveled in the recognition that for me, this was the toughest climb I had faced, but I had made it. Now, I had to recover to be able to finish the race. I sat in the back seat alone feeling sensations slowly return to my hands and feet and worrying that I would have enough energy for my next turn.

Dina had 8 miles to the next vehicle meeting point involving a drop of 1,200 feet and she would take it all the way in. She arrived at the Hancock Time Station at 5:33 am. Our average speed was 13.4 mph. RMC was 1 mph faster. The fastest time recorded for this section since the award was first given, is an impressive 18.35 mph.

Most of the climbing doesn't happen in the West, but in the East. Out of a total of 170,000 feet, 108,000 feet of elevation change has occurred since we crossed the Mississippi River during the last third of the race. By the time we would reach Annapolis, Dina and I had done the lion's share since the Mississippi riding up 67,000 feet of it.

Team B still had some work to do. We were now in Pennsylvania, but were still faced with one last ridgeline to crest. They would be riding up the Buchanan Trail before cresting the ridge and dropping into Cove Gap, the birthplace of the 15th President, James Buchanan. This town was considered America's frontier in 1791 when he was born. Julie and Ann would cover their 52 mile segment in a little over 3 hours at 16 miles per hour.

The climb over Buchanan Trail makes a fitting bookend to Wolf Creek Pass where John Fremont led his survey party to disaster. Fremont would end up as the first candidate nominated by the fledgling Republican Party to run for President in 1856 and his opponent was Buchanan, to whom he would lose.

Despite my exhaustion after the last climb, I couldn't sleep. After getting something to eat, I had climbed into bed and closed my eyes, but sleep didn't come. Part of the reason was the movement of the RV, part of it was the daylight that made it past the closed curtains, but a lot of it was from the excitement of knowing that the worst was over. We still had 180 miles or 10 hours of riding ahead of us, but at this point, it seemed manageable despite the effort I had just expended.

Chapter 20

Final Battlefield

We changed out again in Blue Ridge Summit, PA, at 8:45 am for a 38 mile flat run to Hanover, PA. We were still in rural country with well-tended fields and woodlots. The anticipation of the race finish had reinvigorated me. Once again, my legs were up to the task. Sideling Hill was behind me.

Julie had finished and Dina started our leg. I took over on a short but steep climb, but managed it without much difficulty. Further on, I was back on the bike when we crossed under a covered bridge and when I emerged, views of recently mowed green rolling fields opened up on the other side. It was a welcome sight after the sharp ridges of the prior night. Dina took over just past the bridge by the side of a creek.

Mike got out this time and took my bike to put on the rear rack. I got back in the Audi and grabbed a half of peanut butter and jelly sandwich. The Audi pulled around Dina and the Toyota. Shortly, I heard John's voice on the radio asking for Bill.

"Bill, Amy is up next just before we reach the Gettysburg Park. Dina wants to do the ride through the site. I checked with Joe and he gave it the okay," he said.

It would have been part of my 5 mile section and the idea of riding through the area was just as attractive to me. I told Bill as much.

"John, Amy wants to do the ride. It's her pull." Bill replied.

He was firm. Was he sticking up for me or just being argumentative with John?

Finally a compromise was reached.

"Why don't they both ride it", Bill suggested?

That seemed to be satisfying to everyone, including me. For the last week, except for riding together for a few seconds during exchanges, bumping into each other when we got ready to ride and eating meals at the same table in the RV, we didn't have much interaction. With the race winding down, some camaraderie, some bonhomie given our proximity to the finish seemed in order. I thought of how Julie and Ann linked up riding over the Mississippi River together. We had shared a number of the tough climbs, so a triumphant ride through Gettysburg would be a treat.

I took over for Dina on my third pull near Marsh Creek. After a mile or so into my ride, I passed a sign announcing the Gettysburg National Park. The countryside was a patchwork of mowed fields with woods around the edges. Long stone walls and split rail fences lined the periphery. I could see Dina up the road on her bike looking back in my direction. As I came closer, she started out, I drew alongside and we rode together. On either side of the road were markers for specific battle sites and bronze cannons poking their muzzles through stone walls. We didn't talk to one another as we rode through the Park. It was a good pace, but not a hard pace.

Several miles into our ride, we began a climb into a wooded area that turned out to be Warfield Ridge, the south end of Seminary Ridge where Longstreet staged his fateful attack on Round Top on the second day of the battle. As the road began to climb, Dina popped out of the saddle and began to accelerate dropping me as she did so. I continued on up the hill and made an effort to match her acceleration as she pulled away. But she had opened up a gap that I couldn't close. I rode for another half mile until the Audi pulled up the road in front of me and stopped to pick me up.

Back in the car, I made small talk with Mike about the beautiful day, the scenery and the emotion of the place. Richie's cell phone rang and he answered. He didn't say much, just a lot of " yeah's" and "okay's".

After he finished the call, he turned to me and said," Dave Lyons asked me, to tell you to 'step on it'."

This was a difficult request to understand. Except with Mike and Richie, the dialog that I had with support crew didn't involve much beyond directional guidance, infrequent questions about my condition, some discussion about the distance of each pull and such. Motivational support was measured, particularly with the 2 Daves. I had made an effort to converse with them earlier and Dave Lyons seemed to open up. He chatted about college, his ice hockey team, concerns regarding sports concussions, his child psychiatric practice and how much he enjoyed it. I felt as if we were hinting at a rapport.

Yet when I had finished Sideling Hill, there had been no acknowledgement. And now, his motive for telling me to speed up wasn't obvious. We weren't going to beat team Raw Milk Cats' time. We were way ahead of the other women's team. Where we stood against other teams in the past was not something I was aware of. If there was another time objective, it wasn't mentioned. From Gettysburg, we had another 4 ½ hours to the finish and my share represented maybe an hour of riding and we were already cranking along at 19 mph on increasingly congested roads, how much improvement could be expected?

My thoughts were interrupted by another car honking at us. We were now on a four lane road and had yet to catch up to and pass Dina when another car pulled beside the Audi and the driver honked and waved excitedly. We all looked at one another and tried to figure out who that could be. The Toyota appeared up ahead with Dina in front and our new friend accelerated up to where she was riding and honked and waved excitedly for a second time. Dina looked over and waved back with a big smile. We now had our own horn honking fan section for the ride into Odenton. But somewhere along the line, we lost her and never figured out who she was.

We were to end our ride at a Sheetz Convenience Store in Hanover where we would change teams. But as we approached, there was no RV. Bill called on the radio to determine its location. The RV had taken a separate route from us and had inadvertently gone to the wrong store. They were at a Sheetz, not far away, but at a different address.

We had to keep going.

"Dina and I can finish this section", I said to Richie. "We can take it the rest of the way."

Bill pulled over and I got out to take over for Dina, Mike brought up my bike. While we were waiting, my desire to keep riding was now replaced with a desperate need to take a pee. I gave Mike my bike back and began looking for a hedge or bush to hide behind. He shrugged his shoulders and gestured to ground in front of me and turned his back shielding me. Once again, necessity trumped modesty.

Just then, the RV caught up to us about 5 miles past our officially pre-determined meeting point. Julie scrambled out, and as Dina finished, jumped on her bike to take over on a narrow two lane road with a fair amount of traffic whizzing by.

We had another change upcoming in Mt. Airy, which was back in Maryland. Team B would ride the next 30 miles to get there. The route took them along the old Hanover Pike, which was busy with traffic. The desert, the Rockies the flat plains and farmlands and the punishing finish in the Appalachians were behind us. It seemed annoying, almost an insult, to have to deal with urban crowding, strip malls, traffic and congestion now that we were almost there.

After 8 miles, the route turned southwest at Manchester in a direction away from the finish. The next town we would pass through was Westminster, MD,. The road we were on was a natural corridor which continues on through Mt. Airy and eventually reaches Leesburg, VA .

It was the route used by the Confederate General J.E.B. Stuart and the 5,000 man 4th Virginia Cavalry on their way north to the Gettysburg Battlefield 149 years ago. When the 4th reached Westminster, they were confronted by what became known as, "Corbit's Charge". After hearing that there were Confederate troops in the town, a certain Captain Corbit led 90 Union Cavalry troops in what historians refer to as a 'bravely suicidal' charge into the teeth of Stuart's overwhelming numbers. While he was quickly captured, Corbit's presence so unsettled Stuart that he delayed by a day his arrival at Gettysburg, which many believe had a crucial impact on the outcome of that battle.

The Love Sweat & Gears contingent charged into Westminster on the same road on this final day but was only confronted by a short delay from the traffic light on Main St. Once through town, it was a straight run on Ridge Road, through semi-rural countryside all the way to the Mt. Airy exchange point.

I sat in the RV as it drove there listening to a discussion of how we would organize the finish of the race. Who would be riding, which bikes would be taken, what vehicle would follow and which crew members would be in it? It seemed foreign to have this discussion. That we were close to the finish was at once a relief, but at the same time would end the predictability of the routine we had established over the last 7 days. We would lose the edge for that charge into battle that had become our reason for existence.

At Mr. Airy, if a team had accumulated any time penalties during the race, they are required to wait in a penalty box for the amount of minutes that had been accumulated. We had not been assessed any, so when Ann came in we were free to go. I was up first.

Dina and I had 40 more miles to ride to Odenton. We started out going south, then turned east, back towards the coast. The first half was on relatively flat two lane rural roads, through the Patuxent River Park and over the Triadelphia Reservoir Dam, and for long stretches there were no shoulders. We made good speed on Damascus Road through an area of flat farmland until we hit a number of traffic circle roundabouts and turns. We then crossed into the Patuxent Research Refuge, a thickly wooded area surrounding a facility established by Franklin Roosevelt as the first Federal department to study wildlife and natural resources.

The area we rode through contains archeological sites of early Native Americans going back 10,000 years. Our route also paralleled the Patuxent River, which was explored by Captain John Smith in 1608. He had traveled over 1,000 miles in an open boat exploring and mapping Chesapeake Bay and its rivers and had ventured up many rivers, including the Patuxent, in the belief he could find a passage that would lead to the Pacific Ocean. He didn't find one, and having just left the object of his quest a week ago, I understood only too well why.

I was on the bike when we turned onto a freeway on the southern edge of the Fort Meade cantonment. It had a big wide bicycle lane. I settled into my aero bars, and picked up a good tempo. After several miles, Richie voice came over the loudspeaker.

"Turn right after the bridge toward Odenton".

I looked up, saw the sign on an over pass and the long sweeping turn that followed. We were now on the old Annapolis Road. This would be my last time on the bike before the ceremonial last few miles. I rode hard and despite the increasing congestion, stops and turns we still averaged 18.5 mph exceeding RMC by over 1 mph. We had stepped on it.

Julie and Ann took over in Odenton, and Julie would ride the last section of the race. It was through the suburban sprawl that radiates from Baltimore, Annapolis and Washington, D.C. There was only 9.5 miles of timed riding left which was covered at 11.6 mph, 17 minutes slower than RMC.

The race officially finishes on the Annapolis town dock, but the timed racing ends next to an establishment called the Rams Head Roadhouse. Here teams pick up an escort to follow for the last 6 miles to the finish at a park next to City Dock at a measured pace.

Ann was on the side of the road when Julie crossed the official finish line and threw up her hands in celebration. Dina was next to arrive and I came in behind her in the Audi. Dina and I joined Julie and Ann for a celebratory gathering. Someone had thought to bring a bottle of champagne and glasses, with which to toast one another. It was a joyous moment.

A non-descript white van would be our escort. All four of us got on our bikes and fell in behind as it guided us through the outskirts of Annapolis, then into the city proper. This of course was necessary, but the congestion and the grittiness of the city surroundings stood in contrast to the vast open continent we had just traversed

As we rode, there was lightness to my mood. The pressure was off. The climbs, the heat, the ghostly donkeys, the alligators disguised as dead armadillos, (or was it the other way around), and the trampoline bed in the RV, were in the past. I was happy the race was ending, I was proud of my accomplishment

Everyone talked about how they felt. Julie said she was humbled by what she believed to be a life changing experiencing. It was a statement that lost some of its poignancy when the van we were following made a wrong turn into a shopping mall parking lot, requiring us to circle through before continuing on our way.

When we got closer to the City Dock finishing area, passers-by on the street greeted us with cheers and waves to which we happily responded. We finally reached our destination and entered a lane lined with barriers emblazoned with the RAAM logo. At the end was a finish line under a large Race Across America banner and a small crowd cheering. Here we stopped for pictures. The NBC Nightly News crew was there and Arne got comments from us while the camera recorded the obligatory shrieks and kisses and hugs.

Richie's Dad was there, as was Julie's daughter. Whitney, Dina's partner appeared with a big hand printed "You Did It" sign. She was apparently less athletically inclined than Dina because she kept asking no one in particular, "I don't know why Dina does this, do you? What does she see in this?"

Then we were ushered to a stage under a large white tent where a heavy set man was standing. One by one, he asked us to reflect on our race experience and then did the same thing with some of the crew. More photos with crew, who were all wearing their official red t-shirt and then racers alone. We were then presented with medals. Bill was happy and smiling. I hadn't ruined his RAAM after all.

After the finishing ceremonies, we boarded the RV and left for the motel. When we arrived, I headed for the shower for a good soaking. During the race, water use on the RV was always tricky both from a supply and waste capacity standpoint. Other than sponging off when I washed out my shorts, I had taken only one real shower in the last week and the pleasure of a long soak in streaming hot water was not going to be ignored.

We still had the drive back to Denver. Mike picked through the gear on the RV for our stuff and began loading it in the Toyota, which we were going to drive back to Denver with Richie and his Dad. He also loaded my two bicycles on the top rack.

RAAM organizers do a series of banquets during the week as the various classes of competitors finish. Our banquet included the solo men's and women's overall winners. Then George called us up to give us our awards. He handed out several plaques, one for the team and its placing and one for each individual. We of course finished first as we were the only team in our age group to race.

Our official time was 7 days 36 minutes. It was the second fastest time in the 31 year history of RAAM for a four woman's relay team 50-59 years of age. Of all the women's teams, only one other was close to our time. We beat the 2005 Roaring Fork Volvo B2B Divas, an under 50 year old women's team by 6 minutes, although they did a longer route and averaged 18.09 mph to our 17.75 mph. This was the Divas second year. They had broken the 7 day time barrier in 2004 on a shorter course at a slower 17.69 mph average. As to the team we really wanted to beat, we finished 13 hours and 2 minutes behind Raw Milk Cats. Their 19.02 mph time will be difficult for anyone to overcome.

There should be an asterisk next to our finishing time because it was the fastest ever for a women's 4 person team that included a 60+ rider. Just in case you wondered.

As to the others who raced against us that year, we finished ahead of the only other woman's team by 27 hours. We were actually pretty close in age as they averaged 49.8 years of age to our 53.8. We also finished ahead of 9 other four person men's and mixed teams out of a total of 22.

Despite the disparity over the first two days, the race load in mileage evened out between the two sets of relay partners. Dina and I had ridden 1,485 miles for 86 hours at 17.3 mph while Ann and Julie completed 1,508 miles in 83 hours at 18.1 mph. Dina forwarded her Garmin results showing 46 hours of riding covering 845 miles at 18.4 mph. If correct, that would leave me with 40 hours covering 648 miles at 16.2 mph.

Dina was our youngest rider and proved to be the work horse for the team. She tackled the first 24 miles of the race by herself and worked to take on a lot of the downhill run outs that show up in her distance and speed. But despite fewer miles and less time on the bike, the two of us shared the hard parts.

We survived the death zone, conquered all the high passes of Colorado, fought the winds of Kansas and prevailed on the steep grades of the Appalachians. And while doing so, for our team, we rode the longest legs in time and distance and set the fastest average speed between Time Stations. I would not have tabbed myself as the choice to take the responsibility for as much of the tougher sections that came my way, but I rode them. Each time it was required for me to get on my bike and ride; I got on my bike and I rode.

It wasn't easy. It wasn't always pretty. There was a little of the making of sausage cliché associated with this event. One wouldn't really want to know all that went into it. Differences of opinion did occur. Other RAAM racers I have spoken to have expressed conflicted views in their response to the "How'd it go?" question. There have been incidences in past RAAMs when relations on the teams got so bad that crews quit mid-race and left their riders stranded. Yet despite the issues, Love, Sweat & Gears did a good RAAM. Joe acted the adult and brought a level of maturity to the affair. And, in the end, we posted a terrific time against unfavorable winds. The crew did their jobs efficiently, responded well to solving problems, kept our exchanges smooth and didn't run us over. What more can you ask? Hats off to them.

I did not bring my Garmin to record my results. In retrospect, if I had, it would have given me a more accurate reading. But at the time, after 15 months of downloading data into my computer and waiting for the workout to turn green or red, I didn't want to be encumbered.

Inevitably, we all end up looking at individual performance as a measure of achievement. And while a rider's speed, or a team's overall time versus another, gives us one way to measure such a race, it can never render an accurate reading of what was accomplished.

Before the race started, there was a point of view that I was the weakest rider. Yet I proved to myself that "weak" was not a description to which I answered. The satisfaction I took from conquering Hayman and Oak Creek in the heat, the elation after cresting Cucharas, the thrill of the speeds we hit coming into Walsh, the emotional highs of El Dorado and Hamel, and the pride in summiting Sideling Hill are not digitally measurable, but they were nonetheless part of my score.

The race proved to be every bit a great adventure; a journey across America few will ever experience in a similar manner. For over a year, I had three elephants standing on my toes, and when the gun went off and Dina started out, I still had one left. Could I get back on the bike time and again, day and night? Could I deal with that last elephant?

Could I do it?

As Mike would say, "Yes, you can."

•

A week after the end of the race, I scheduled a stand up paddleboard lesson on Soda Lake in Denver's Bear Creek Park and shortly thereafter got my own board.

I continued my career of selling real estate. The following summer, I returned to the water to row and finished the season with another gold medal in a hard fought woman's quadruple sculls event at the FISA Masters Regatta in Varese, Italy. In addition, after a 15 year hiatus, and in a test of marital harmony, Mike and I enjoyed good results rowing a mixed double at a couple local regattas including the 14 mile Horse Tooth Ache Race.

Dina returned to her work at ARUP Labs, had hip replacement surgery, then got back on the bike to train for the Furnace Creek 508 endurance race, which passes through Death Valley. Due to flood damage it was cut to 353 miles and called the TRONA 353. She won the woman's overall title in 23 hours 22 minutes.

Ann and Julie retained the Love Sweat & Gears name, recruited two younger professional cyclists and tried RAAM again, finishing 7 hours short of the Raw Milk Cats record.

At the 2013 Colorado Sportswomen of the Year Award Banquet, Ann, Julie and I accepted the Swede Johnson Spirit Award given to Love Sweat & Gears for their Race Across America success.

After battling cancer, Fuzzy Mitchell passed away. He had raced RAAM 3 times, was part of a 75 and over, record holding, 4 man relay team and was a Crew Chief for endurance cyclists on dozens of other occasions. His like will not soon be seen again.

On September 19, 2013, Death Valley claimed another victim. Chuck Caha, was repairing flood damage with a road grader, when a tire went flat. He tried to walk 5 miles back to his pickup truck but died before reaching it from a heat stroke in triple digit temperatures. He was the same age as I am.

Bibliography;

Wikipedia was our source for much of the historical information included in this book. However, we did review the following for additional detail.

Lightfoot, Kent G. (2004). <u>Indians, Missionaries, and Merchants: The Legacy of Colonial Encounters on the California Frontiers</u>. University of California Press, Berkeley, CA

Hafen, Leroy; David Dary (2004). <u>The Overland Mail, 1849-1969: Promoter of Settlement Precursor of Railroads</u>.: University of Oklahoma Press.

Juan Batista de Anza Dairies, University of Oregon,

von Voightlander , Karl, Borrego's Christmas Angel, December, 1964, Desert Magazine.

Parker, Arthur (1919). <u>The Life of General Ely S. Parker</u>. Buffalo Historical Society

<u>Men to Match My Mountain</u>, Irving Stone, page 173

<u>Contested Space: Mormons, Navajos, and Hopis in the Colonization of Tuba City</u>, Corey Smallcanyon, BYU

Simmons, Virginia McConnell. Ute Indians of Utah, Colorado, and New Mexico. Norman: University of Oklahoma Press*Pioneer Women, Joanna L Stratton, page 124*

Rolle, Andrew (1991). John Charles Frémont: Character as Destiny. Norman: University of Oklahoma Press

Perkins, James E. (1999). Tom Tobin: Frontiersman. Herodotus Press

DeArment, Robert K. Bat Masterson: The Man and the Legend. University of Oklahoma Press

Neeley, Bill (September 2009). The Last Comanche Chief: The Life and Times of Quanah Parker Castle Books.

Women on the American Frontier, William Fowler

Judy Rosella Edwards, Ada Kepley Biography, Unitarian Universalist Historical Society.

James M. Collins, The Archaeology of the Cahokia Mounds, Springfield IL, Illinois Historic Preservation Agency (1990)

About the Author

Michael Shonstrom was born and raised in Pasadena, California, attended Pomona College, graduated from UCLA in 1961 and earned a Master's of Business Administration Degree from Columbia University Graduate School of Business in 1965.

He began a career in the securities industry in New York where he became Vice President of Institutional Research with Faulkner, Dawkins & Sullivan. He subsequently owned and operated a country inn and adventure tour organizer in Vermont before returning to provide security analysis for several firms, including his own, and recently retired from a position as Director of Equity Research at GVC Capital in Denver.

Team 411/Love Sweat & Gears: Dina, Ann, Julie and Amy after receiving medals at the finishing line in Annapolis, Maryland 6/23/2012

48885988R00106

Made in the USA
Middletown, DE
29 September 2017